D1176925

MY FIRST TIME

A COLLECTION OF FIRST PUNK SHOW STORIES

WITHDRAWN FOR FREE USE IN CITY
CULTU... INSTITUTIONS
MAY ... THE BENEFIT OF
THE NEW YORK PUBLIC LIBRARY ONLY.

MY FIRST TIME

A COLLECTION OF FIRST PUNK SHOW STORIES

EDITED BY CHRIS DUNCAN

PRESS

EDINBURGH · OAKLAND · WEST VIRGINIA

My First Time: A Collection of First Punk Show Stories
©2007 Chris Duncan
© This edition published by AK Press, 2007

ISBN 9781904859178

A catalog record is available for this title from the Library of Congress.
Library of Congress Control Number: 2006933526

AK Press
674-A 23rd Street
Oakland, CA 94612
USA
www.akpress.org
akpress@akpress.org

AK Press
PO Box 12766
Edinburgh, EH8 9YE
Scotland
www.akuk.com
ak@akedin.demon.co.uk

The above addresses would be delighted to provide you with the latest AK
Press distribution catalog, which features the several thousand books, pam-
phlets, zines, audio and video products, and stylish apparel published and/or
distributed by AK Press. Alternatively, visit our website for the complete
catalog, latest news, and secure ordering.

Printed in Canada on acid free, recycled paper with union labor.
Cover design by Brett Critchlow (www.juicedesign.com).
Cover photo by Schledewitz.

Acknowledgments

This book was initially going to be a zine made in an edition of fifty: photo-copied, hand-numbered, a silkscreened cover with the title in pretty script—or something of that nature—and ten stories at best. The idea came as I was exiting art college in 2003. School is a place that piles projects on you, and when school ends you have to pile projects on yourself. So it started...but it quickly got put on the backburner as other projects came about and seemed more pressing. Also, being at the mercy of other people is hard, as anyone who's has ever tried to organize and gather knows what I'm talking about.

Fast forward to 2006. My friend Zach Blue (one of the folks whom I had asked to write a story for me a year before) at AK Press called and asked if I was still collecting stories. I was, kind of. He said AK would be interested in publishing it if I was game, so here we are. That started a long process of reaching out to all the generations of the punk community we could find. This is what we came up with. I would like to thank Zach for lighting a fire under me and forcing me to make it happen through a truly weird time in my life. I would also like to thank Scott Bourne and Blake Schwarzenbach for being the first two folks to send me stories for the "zine" I was going to do.

At the very last minute, we reached out for photos of bands to accompany some of the stories, and Adam Tanner and Al Quint stepped up and made it happen. I have also had the pleasure of working with Brett Critchlow at Juice Design over the years and was very happy that he agreed to design the cover of *My First Time*.

I hope everyone enjoys the efforts of this book. Feel free to send your first show story here: christopherrobinduncan@gmail.com.

—Chris Duncan

...I BELIEVE IN MOMENTS, TRANSPARENT MOMENTS, MOMENTS IN GRACE WHEN YOU HAVE TO STAKE YOUR FAITH

—RITES OF SPRING

...WE WERE FUCKING CORN-DOGS

—MINUTEMEN

CONTENTS

INTRODUCTION

Chris Duncan

The first thing I did was brace myself. I don't know what else I could have done. By the time I could make sense of what was happening, it was over; the bands were packing up, my life had shifted, and I was in the "back seat" of a red 1986 Honda Civic hatch-back, leaving Norwalk, heading south towards Jersey, sweaty and wide-eyed and crammed in the backseat—on fire—with a friend whose name has escaped me. After all, it's been almost twenty years.

There's something about beginnings, something magical and romantic and completely ridiculous. There is something dangerous as well. As humans, how often do we discover something that completely changes our lives? How often can we pinpoint the exact moment when you know, down deep in your guts, that things can never ever be the same again? One second it's okay to swallow the soulless spoonfuls of popular culture, and with a flick of a switch, a whole new world opens up, so much so that just the sound of Def Leppard or Lionel Richie or the Eagles or the Grateful Dead acutely resembles fingernails on a chalkboard.

I think youthful idealism is beautiful. The urgency and power that a group of humans with the same beliefs and ideas can harness is intoxicating and infectious. I think that's what does it; that unified/unifying urgency is what makes people invest their lives and take ownership of a scene, sub-culture, or identity, even though eventually they may drift from the community they helped construct. The ability to participate and build, rather than just plainly observe and accept without question, is what's key. It's about being in a place so intimate that just showing up makes you an integral part of the whole. Knowing that without you, it couldn't be the same. Knowing you are connected to a community.

This book captures the very beginning of that process. These stories are a window into the world(s) of folks who were there—wherever "there" was for them. It starts with some form of discontent (whether boredom or a broken home) that brings the author to a place that is scary, exciting, and new, and ends at a crossroads: the place where sound and fury merge. These stories are more than just intimate, awkward moments of one person's development. As important—and hilarious and interesting—as these personal glimpses are, these stories are also a snapshot from different vantage points of a culture and movement that affected people so deeply, politicizing them, making them feel they belonged somewhere. These pieces put the history of a time and place, so often expressed only verbally, into writing, and let us share events experienced first-hand by only a few. They shine a light into hole-in-the-wall pubs in England, dive bars in the South, and legendary music venues, illuminating the dorks, nerds, weirdos, and outcasts who were all on the verge of finding a place where it was ok. Where it would be ok. Where people just like them invented the music, the records, the publications, the styles and attitudes; those things they identified with so closely, those things that eventually felt like home. An umbrella from the status quo, their perceived differentness, and their dissatisfaction.

Like just about everyone else on the planet, I was a messed up kid. By the time I could have been good at sports I already hated them: I had an inability to relate to the jocks—and them to me; a distaste for hitting balls with sticks or kicking them with my feet; and a disgust of the testosterone-driven behaviors that seemed to come with high school sports. I was searching for something, and I developed an interest in the weirdness and individuality (or what seemed like it at the time) of skate-boarding and strange music and funny haircuts.

It was 1987, and much to my mother's dismay, I jumped into the back of a friend's car to head two hours north to a venue called the Anthrax, in Norwalk, CT. We left around 6 pm and wouldn't return until 4 o'clock the next morning. My life had changed. My mother was not pleased.

There was a mixed tape that always found its way into the boombox at the slappy curb in my neighborhood. That tape was an entry point to the shows I would see (my first was Gorilla Biscuits and Sick of it All), and it opened my eyes (and ears) to the music I would end up listening to for years to come.

These days, I think what interests me most about any sort of subcul-ture—or development within a subculture—is the act of discovery. In a Google-driven world does that really even exist anymore? Do people still discover and learn things by their personal experience? We live in a time when anyone who has access to a computer and a topic in mind can easily pull up articles and images to satisfy their curiosity. Despite the Internet's obvious benefits, one could argue that, at least culturally, it risks reducing personal growth and development through first hand experience to a sort of synthesized lifestyle. In the place of social interaction and stomach-churning first times, we have a sea of silent observers, faces lit by LED screens. Pre-Internet discovery was a much different experience. The trial and error and embarrassment endured, led eventually to maturation, growth, and understanding—all earned by living. For me, that's what makes these stories so special. They chronicle those experiences, that journey of discovery, when you find something and make it yours.

MY FIRST SHOW

Boff Whalley

"Mum, I want to learn to use the sewing machine."

A pause—a humming, discernible pause—numb, dumb silence, eyebrows arched, hands on hips.

"You want what?"

"To learn to use the sewing machine."

"…Why do you want to learn how to use a sewing machine?"

"To take in some trousers."

And then the pause is longer, more careful. It's a thinking pause, a knowing pause. My mum's heard me talking about this "punk" thing.

"I'm not helping you to take in your trousers so tight that you cut off your blood circulation."

So this is how it began. Stitch by stitch, leg by leg. Before I'd ever seen a punk band, I'd read about them, heard about them, seen them on TV—The Sex Pistols' first TV appearance on my local telly show, singing

"Anarchy In The UK," shocking the living daylights out of me—and I'd decided, somehow, that this was for me. This was it. I'd spent years trying to find some sort of expression for my rebellion. In small town Burnley, Lancashire, it just wasn't there. Really. I wasn't anti-social, and therefore had no desire to express rebellion by stealing handbags and setting fire to school buildings. I wasn't stupid, so couldn't channel anger into football violence or bullying. And so it came by taking in my own trousers, turning flares into drainpipes, stitch by stitch, leg by leg.

This was the way. Make yourself look stupid. Have people point at you in the street. I learnt how to use the sewing machine; my older sister taught me. My first pair of homemade trousers was made from Superman curtain material.

For a while it seemed like I lived from 7" single to 7" single. There was nothing else. I lived in the north west of England; I had to get on a bus for an hour to Manchester to buy the records that began the soundtrack to my life. Pistols, Damned, Buzzcocks, Adverts, and then suddenly a rush, a push, and a thousand others.

But shows? There were no shows in our town. Nobody played in Burnley. Not yet.

A band started. Kev Hemingway, the first boy at our school to dye his hair, was the singer for a very short while. They practiced at a youth club for four or five months, then Kev took up the drums. Sage, one of my best mates, played guitar. Haggis, cocky and funny, became the singer. Roger, older and able to play keyboards, wrote the songs. They called themselves Notsensibles and arranged a gig at the Youth Club.

A punk gig? In our town? It was an event that would be remembered in terms completely and utterly out of proportion to the facts surrounding it: local punk band, first gig, youth club, half-empty audience, weird clothes, ten o'clock curfew.

But this was where I discovered a new world. And looking around at the time, I really did sense that those around me knew about this new world too. Years later I discovered that this was true—this was a turning point. People who'd survived in small cliques, who'd argued with their parents about using the sewing machine, who'd thought they were stranded and alienated, suddenly felt a local camaraderie: a sense of community.

Notsensibles were (of course) shoddy and sloppy, out-of-tune and under-rehearsed. But they were inspirational, shocking and defiant, too.

Within a year they'd learnt how to tune up, how to play in time, how to write good songs. But that night, their amateur efforts, their crap clothes, and that sense of "we're doing this thing, whatever it is, and you know what—it could be you!" was overwhelmingly inspiring and exciting. Punk, with its "anyone can start a band" spirit had been, before this, nothing more than a glamorous London-based ethos. Now it was a reality. It was true—anyone could do it! Amazing.

Secretly (or was it obvious?) I wanted to be in Notsensibles. I couldn't believe I wasn't part of that band. They were so inspiring. They were my mates! The punk ethos said, "Why couldn't I just join in?" But they didn't need anyone else, so I decided I had to go and do it myself. Such was the impact of that show. After this concert there came a flood of punk gigs and shows in the area. Suddenly there was a community of punks: girls and boys who'd learned how to use a sewing machine, girls and boys who created their own shows, followed the bands, and went on to other things.

But that was the night that clinched it. A small youth club in Burnley, Lancashire, some bunch of strangely dressed teenagers playing the Adverts' "One Chord Wonders" incredibly badly. Oh, epiphany, joy, illumination, and onward to the rest of my life. Bring it on. If anything could be as weird and wonderful as this, then… then set up that sewing machine. Stitch by stitch, leg by leg. Drrrrrrrrrrrrrrrrrrrrrrrrrrrrrrrrrrrrrrrrrrrrrrr rrrrrrrrrrrrrrrrrrrrrrrrrrrrrrrrrrrrrrrrrrrrrrrrrrrrrrrrrrrrrrrrrrrrrrrrrrrr rrrrrrrrrrrrrrrrrrrrrrrrrrrrrrrrrrrrrrrrrrrrrrrrrrrrrrrrrrrrrrrrrrrrrrrrrrrr rrrr

CAN I JOIN THE HIGH RANKS OF THE LOW LIFES NOW?

Andrew Scott

My first punk show was, retrospectively, not especially mind-blowing. What makes it stand out was that it was my first show and I was nervous as hell. It was more of something that I had to do, rather than something I wanted to do. The act of attending punk shows was a socially enforced rite of passage in my high school. Basically, it worked like this: if one wore band t-shirts, hung out with punk rockers, and didn't go to shows, they were heckled, labeled as a "poser," and cast to the bottom rung in the pecking order. No one wanted to be there. In the cruel and delicate natural selection that embodies the social politics of youth, the bottom wrung is an ugly place. It was a pariah-like social class that was denied entry into backyard skate ramps, car rides, being with girls, and anything that makes high school at all bearable. In order to avoid this tragic fate, and thus graduate into the higher ranks of the social outcasts, one had to prove that they were authentically punk rock by going to shows. The older punks enforced this unspoken rule with an iron fist, either get in there and participate...or face the consequences. So I, somewhat reluctantly, went to my first punk rock show.

The year was 1987. A friend's mom gave us a ride down to the city and hesitantly dropped us off at a club on Chicago's north side. We stepped out of the car and into a line of freaks streaming into the front doors of the Cabaret Metro. Walking up the stairs that led into the main room, we managed to lose each other in the crowd. My friend was nowhere to be found. I was alone in a room of strangers and it was a bit unnerving. The tension in the air was as palpable as the cigarette smoke that filled the room. Something big was about to happen and I could feel it. Wading through a sea of mohawks, studded leather jackets, and combat boots, the lights dimmed and the chitter-chatter turned to hoots and hollers. Jeff Pezzati walked onto the stage of the crowded, sweaty auditorium, grabbed the microphone, and said, "Hi, we're Naked Raygun." And then without a word, it all happened.

Giant amplifiers blasted out a raunchy chord, followed by a machine gun drumbeat. The crowd erupted. I was swallowed into a barrage of arms, legs, and punkish shrapnel. I couldn't see anything amidst the mass of humanity that I was floating around in, but I could certainly hear every ear-splitting power-chord coming from the stage. As the band sang, the entire crowd flipped out, shouting every word with fists in the air: "We could use...the RAT PATRO-OH-OLE!!!" Beneath my Vans, the wooden floor of the old auditorium flexed under the intense weight of the crowd. I kept thinking, "Oh my God, we're all gonna die." Except no one besides me seemed to notice—or care—and the band played on. Bodies were flying everywhere—stage-diving, crowd-surfing—and I was lost at sea, being spun, pushed, pulled, and knocked around in the melee. Forty-five minutes later, as the band ended its set, I was finally spit out of the swarming ball. I was terrified. My heart was pounding, my body was bruised beyond belief, but my mind was spinning with more emotions than I could make sense of. I just kept thinking, "Holy fuck!" The catharsis of dancing, the deafeningly loud music, the multiple near-death experiences...The whole scene was more than my thirteen-year-old mind could comprehend. It freaked me out, but at the same time, something about it was invigorating. Regardless of the peer pressures that caused me to attend this show, I loved it and would definitely be back for more.

Attending shows became a major part of my life in the years that followed. Every weekend was filled with trips to see random bands at some club, basement, or VFW hall in the urban sprawl of Chicago. I was eventually accepted into the skate punk clique by the older kids and was able to skate their backyard ramps, got a girlfriend, and found shelter from the jocks. Eventually, I got older and found myself calling the younger kids posers. I hazed them as the older kids had me, demanding that they too participate...And thus the cycle continued.

THE NIGHT I ALMOST TOOK A DIVE

Andy Shoup

I ran away from home to go to my first punk show. It was Friday, May 17, 1985. I still have the flyer. The show took place at the Crest Theatre in Sacramento. D.O.A played, as well as the Circle Jerks, the Fastbacks, Tales of Terror, and Problem Fish.

At the time, I lived in Modesto, California and was fourteen years old. I was dating my first girlfriend, Sylvia, who looked a little like Pat Benatar. She was trouble and my parents knew it: she was a dropout, and three years older than me. Sylvia tried to kiss-up to my parents, but she only ended up coming off like Eddie Haskell.

Sylvia's friend, Mary Ann, drove us to the show in a beat up, two-door, yellow Oldsmobile. We got to Sacramento at dusk. All of the punks, skinheads, and freaks were hanging out in front of the Crest Theatre— and all over the K Street Mall.

I remember what I was wearing because, like most punks, I planned my outfits carefully. I had on a Corrosion of Conformity "Eye for an Eye" t-shirt, ripped black jeans, and hi-top Vans with black and white stripes. I was definitely trying to look cool, but without standing out too much. I was the perfect blend of rebel and wuss.

Before the show, Sylvia and Mary Ann and I were hanging out, goofing around, when this bunch of skate-punks cruised by.

"Hey," one of them called out, "that kid looks like Amy Shoup's little brother."

They circled around and came over to say hi.

"What the fuck are you doing here, ya little shit?" said a guy named Sten. "Your parents let you out of the house? I heard you ran away last week."

"Yeah," I said, "and *this* week."

"Alright, grommet," said Sten, "have fun."

Sten and his buddies skated off and I basked in the elation that came with being given the time of day by dudes who were four years older than I was, and who were exponentially cooler than anyone my age—or so it seemed at the time. "We should go in pretty soon," said Sylvia, "so we don't miss Problem Fish."

Problem Fish were our hometown heroes—and the main reason that most of the Modesto punks came out on that night. They were a pretty basic three-chord '80s punk band, with the added benefit of being odd in ways that are hard to describe (including their tendency to insert saxophone solos into hardcore songs). They were sort of nerdy, took lots of acid, and all lived in a dark, musty apartment off an alley in downtown Modesto called the Serf Kitchen. They were also really nice at a time when a lot of the punks were doing their best to scare and intimidate little posers like me.

The best thing, though, was that they were *our* band. I saw them play countless times throughout the '80s, but this was their most exciting show. I mean, D.O.A.? The Circle Jerks? Those bands were fucking heavy hitters. I even dug Tales of Terror, with their sloppy, metallic skate rock sound. They were emblematic of that time: all crazy and wasted and flaunting an excessive metal aesthetic that pissed off the purists, but entertained most everyone else.

We made our way into the Crest Theatre as Problem Fish was playing their best-known song, "Pigs in Drag," to a crowd of maybe sixty people. The Crest is huge, with rows and rows of seats, balconies, and a giant orchestra pit. From the balcony, sixty people looked like a few scattered little ants.

Problem Fish put on a good show, but the pit was mostly filled with the punks who had made the drive up from Modesto. The Fastbacks were up next, but they did little more to really get the crowd going.

When Tales of Terror hit the stage, shit really started going crazy. Their singer, Rat's Ass, was doing terrible back flips off the kick drum, all the while swigging copious amounts of Rainier Beer. Every time he got most of the way through a can, he would whiz it through the air and grab another. One of the cans hit me in the head. I grabbed it, and held on to it, keeping it for years afterwards. The next thing to hit me in the head was an engineer boot, which was worn by a stage-diving Marian Holloway (later Marian Anderson, singer of the Insaints). A Modesto native, Marian was a large woman, probably 6'2". She knocked me completely on my ass, and yes, it hurt.

That show was complete mayhem—it was such a different time. I can't really remember any security guards being there. I do, however, remember almost everybody smoking (in a huge, darkened, art deco theater, mind you), dudes skateboarding down the aisles, and it seemed like most everyone had brought in their own 12-pack.

D.O.A. took to the stage and completely destroyed. They played the anti-Ronald Reagan song, "Fucked up Ronnie," and everyone went nuts— Reagan was still in office and we all hated his guts. All of us, except for the Nazi skins that is, and they were in attendance that night, *sieg heiling* and being generally stupid, although terrifying.

Then the Circle Jerks came on. After their first song, Keith Morris took a break from singing and started a long-winded diatribe. I seized the opportunity to go use the bathroom.

When I came back, I felt inspired to stage-dive. The stage was high but didn't look all that hard to climb on to, judging by the number of people who had been stage-diving over the last two bands' sets. Most people were getting caught and buoyed up by the crowd—or at least their return to Earth was somewhat cushioned by some unsuspecting spectator. Plus, no one else was going for it! It was like it was constantly my turn!

There was a little voice in my head that kept saying, "DO IT! DO IT! DO IT!" I was in and around the pit for most of the Circle Jerks set, trying furiously to psych myself up to actually take the plunge.

The thing was, though, as much fun as a stage-dive seemed, I was still, for the most part, a total wuss. So, at the risk of letting myself down, I decided that stage-diving was not in the cards for that evening and returned to cuddle with Sylvia high in the balcony seats, as the pit below revolved and writhed to the strains of "Red Tape" and "World up my Ass."

Soon it was time to go. We took our time filtering out of the Crest and into the streets, downing a couple more beers before we made the drive back to Modesto.

On the way out to the car Sylvia said, "Wasn't it cool how Keith Morris made that speech about how he almost broke his neck stage-diving, and then he asked the crowd to not stage-dive during their set, and then no one did? Wasn't that great?"

This was the diatribe that Keith Morris had started in on as I headed for the bathroom.

"Uhhhh, yeah Sylvia," I said, "that was pretty cool."

It's impossible to say whether the show was such a blast because I was so young, or on the run, or because the bands were so good, or any combination of the above. It is only certain that that show will live forever in my mind as an example of how ridiculously fun punk rock can be. It's an example of how you can think the world works within certain constraints—according to certain rules—and then all of a sudden, you are exposed to a new environment that makes you feel like everything you knew before can get chucked right out the fucking window, and from that point on, you want only to think about the New Way.

WHAT DO YOU CALL THAT NOISE? QU'EST-CE QUE C'EST? THIS IS [ART] POP, YEAH, YEAH!

Jack Rabid

My first punk show was a rather remarkable one: Talking Heads and XTC at Beacon Theater in New York in 1978. OK, some might consider that a "New Wave" show these days, but at the time, any kind of underground expression of this sort of edge was considered "punk," and I thought that was a much more healthy and open-minded idea/ideal.

I was sixteen and on one of my first "dates." I took this girl Diana Mallows into the city from my suburban NJ town, Summit. From Hoboken, we took the Path train and then the subway up to the Upper West Side. All this sounds commonplace now, but it could feel pretty scary then, even for someone much older and experienced than I. Bankrupt, poor, crime-ridden, and filthy, New York in the late-70s (see the fun new book, *Ladies and Gentlemen, The Bronx is Burning*, about 1977 New York), was as much of the exotic "punk" experience to me as putting on my Sex Pistols shirt and Clash buttons and spiking my hair for the occasion. And this was also my first "rock" concert of any kind, so my personal thrill level was off the meter when I scalped a pair of front row tickets right out in front of the venue for like $40. Wow! What a night!

I snuck in a bottle of red wine I had hidden down my pants (funny, I know), so that Diana and I could get pretty buzzed for the show. Looking back, I could have just done it on sheer adrenaline.

My best friend Dave Stein freeloaded a spot with us by sitting at my feet, in the little aisle between the seats and the stage. Considering how excited I was, it is regrettable that I didn't enjoy XTC that much—as they later became one of my favorite bands—but then again, I don't listen to that original Barry Andrews-era, first two-LPs lineup much these days. I liked the energy, and thought they were visually excellent. A few songs, like "This is Pop," I remember favoring, making me think that I should keep an eye on them—which ended up in my great love of *Drums and Wires* the next year and *Black Sea* two years later.

But Talking Heads! Man they were tight, spiky, weird, paranoid, bizarrely business-like, and strangely amazing. (I found out later David Byrne was on coke all the time: explains a lot.) They were supporting *More Songs About Buildings and Food* (which is when I think they really peaked). Songs like "The Girls Just Want to Be With the Girls" pounded into my brain about six times louder than I ever suspected it would. At one point Byrne even asked me a question. (Dumbfounded, I pointed to myself—"me?"—and found that the cliché that punk had done away with the fourth wall was so true). But the greatest thing was how there was ZERO concession to the whole idea of them being Vegas-esque "entertainers." There was no "How are you New York!?" or "Are you having a good time!?" or introducing the members or anything, but the music, music, music. And I remember thinking how astonishingly revolutionary that was compared to the awful drek I'd endured, with what little live rock there was on TV back then—on *Don Kirshner's Rock Concert* or *The Midnight Special*, if my parents were out of town and I could sneak staying up that late.

"Artists Only" and especially "The Big Country" just blew my mind with how insidiously subversive they felt, even without the sheer blasting volume of my other favorite bands of the time like Buzzcocks, Rezillos, X-Ray Spex, and the recently defunct The Damned. "Psycho Killer" felt hair-raising, and "Take Me to the River" felt as cool and graceful as Al Green's original. I was edified both personally and culturally. I went home determined to see every concert that I was dying to see from then on. For the last twenty-eight years I have done exactly that—a couple of thousand of them! And I still feel that way on the best nights!

JACKIE WAS A PUNK

Jillian Lauren

Jackie was a punk, the genuine article. I met her at a summer program for arty-type kids, which was held at a prestigious women's college in Western Massachusetts complete with a lush, green campus and all the ceramics classes you could ever want. I went there because I needed to escape my small town in New Jersey. I felt I had been dropped into Livingston from another planet. I was friendless and odd; the girl who made my own clothes and hung out alone, reading in my room. It was 1986, the summer I turned thirteen. As the crowning humiliation of junior high school, I had recently suffered through my Bat Mitzvah while drowning in about fifty yards of pink taffeta. I was ripe for reinvention.

I wasn't entirely clueless. My older cousin, who had a fondness for vintage lunchboxes and combat boots, had introduced me to the Ramones and The Sex Pistols. The infectious energy had captivated me immediately. I was one t-shirt and two LPs into my punk career. I was wearing my treasured Ramones "Rocket to Russia" t-shirt the day I met Jackie.

I had badgered my mother into buying that shirt when I saw it hanging in the window of a tiny record store in New York. After I whined for two full cross-town blocks, she grabbed my hand, turned back around, and marched into the store with me.

My mother can be a trooper. Then-president of the New Jersey chapter of The National Council of Jewish Women, she stared down the sulky clerk who was wearing a purple mohawk flanked on either side by a swastika tattoo.

"She shouldn't have a haircut like that with such a fat face. It's not flattering," had been my mother's final proclamation on the subject, as we walked out onto the street, Ramones t-shirt triumphantly in hand.

So that was the shirt I was wearing when I spotted Jackie walking across the common while looking intently down at the clunky camera that was hanging around her neck. Jackie had red, fried hair: Manic Panic, Pillar Box Red. She sported dark, pegged jeans and a worn "London Calling" t-shirt with a flannel over the top. On her feet were white Chuck Taylors crowded with Sharpie scrawl: Exploited, Cro-Mags, Dead Milkmen, DK, Black Flag, anarchy symbols. There was a chain around her neck with a little silver lock and she slouched as she walked, occasionally looking up from under her hair with black-rimmed eyes. I had never seen anything like her—not close enough to touch and talk to, at least. I had only seen kids like that sitting on stoops in New York. I always secretly yearned to be them instead of me as I walked by, shuffling glumly behind my parents.

The most amazing thing happened between Jackie and me. We became friends. We had so much in common: we hated all the same phony people, we loved the Ramones, we agreed that the only acceptable nail polish color was Wet and Wild black. I impressed her with a flair for exactly recreating the eye makeup Siouxsie wore in a picture in one of Jackie's zines.

Jackie was way ahead of me, and she was way serious about music. She brought a duffel bag full of cassettes for the short three-week stay at the college. We lay head to foot on Jackie's bed in the dorm and stared at the water stained ceiling while we listened to The Clash, The Damned and, my favorite, X. We listened to Dag Nasty and Minor Threat. Jackie told me there were also hardcore bands from Jersey. The Misfits were from Jersey, as well as Patti Smith and Debbie Harry. I wasn't the only one.

That summer I learned that other people felt as angry and alienated as I did, but they weren't killing themselves, as I had often contemplated. Instead they were making music.

Jackie lived in Manhasset, Long Island. At the end of the three weeks we left on buses going in two different directions. I was tearful, but she wasn't; Jackie wasn't a tearful kind of girl. Instead, she gave me her prized Ramones guitar pick on a chain, which I promised to wear without fail. She told me I could come visit her and we'd take the train into the city to see shows.

I was sure that I'd never hear from Jackie again, but I was wrong: a week later I received a letter from her in the mail with my name on the envelope, elaborately lettered in black ballpoint pen. It was a long, conversational letter peppered with little illustrations that picked up where we left off. Jackie concluded the letter with an invitation to visit her in Manhasset. She detailed secret arrangements to escape to the city and meet with some cute, straight edge skaters she knew who hung out in Tompkins Square Park. She had plans for us to go to NaNa and Bleecker Bob's and St. Mark's Place. Of course, I neglected to mention any of these things when I talked my parents into letting me go to spend a weekend with Jackie.

I love train rides. Something about the rapidly rolling landscape and the hum of the engine and the rocking of the train makes me understand writing music. About a half hour into the trip I could feel it. How people make songs out of nothing, out of the air, out of just themselves. I can never hear the music in my head when I am standing still, only when I am moving fast to somewhere new.

Jackie said her mom was cool. So cool, in fact, that she was never around. And Jackie's dad didn't live with them, so instead, she picked me up at the train station with an older friend of hers named Tara. Tara was a petite, responsible punk girl with natural blonde hair that she wore all shaved except for bangs in the front and two long pieces that hung in front of her ears. In the car, Jackie leaned over into the back seat and drew an X with a Sharpie on the top of each of my hands.

"We don't drink, we don't smoke, we don't do drugs, and we don't eat meat," she explained.

"We don't?" I asked.

"We're not sheep," added Tara. "We don't sleep-walk through our lives like zombies."

The no drinking rule seemed extreme to me. Like, why would I ever want to not drink? Filching samples of alcohol out of my parents' liquor cabinet was up there on my list of favorite things to do. But I was ready to try anything. I reasoned that it was cool to not be a sheep. Maybe, if I stuck with Jackie, I wouldn't feel a compelling desire to sleep through my life.

The three of us rode the train to Penn Station late that afternoon. The minute I stepped onto the platform the sweet and stale smell of it hit me, like honey-roasted peanuts and urine mixed together. We flowed into the river of people and I felt crazy alive. The urban gods infused me with pace and attitude, and I was suddenly unafraid of the potential dangers of the New York streets.

We opted for a low-budget vegan meal of two large pretzels split between us, then negotiated the rat maze of tunnels to find the subway line that would take us downtown. Holding onto the sweaty poles of the crowded train, Jackie and Tara explained to me that they were flexible and open-minded. They didn't only see straight edge bands. They didn't participate in that kind of factioning. They told me we were headed to Irving Plaza to see an all-ages show of Murphy's Law, Underdog, and the Dickies. I nodded and pretended like I understood the foreign language they were speaking. I was wearing a mixture of Jackie's clothes and mine: a short, red kilt and fishnets of mine, with a Token Entry t-shirt and Doc Marten boots that belonged to Jackie. I had stepped into a whole new skin.

Irving Plaza is a magical, grungy old theater, and I felt like the queen of the punk prom as we ascended the red-carpeted staircase. Inside was a petri dish of milling young punks, skaters, and skinheads. Tara floated off to find her boyfriend, but first she gave me a quick lecture on the other punks. There were signals you could read in their laces, braces, and tattoos. She clued me in on the rules about which boys it was okay to talk to and which boys it was definitely not.

The room was a blur of exotic tribes with multi-colored hair. There were hundreds of kids there and none looked like anyone in Livingston, New Jersey. They were infinitely more beautiful and fascinating. I felt vindicated. I had just walked through the door I had been waiting for.

Underdog opened the show and the manic wave of sound blasted me back a step. The pit erupted instantly into frenetic writhing. Jackie stood at the perimeter about two rows back from the pandemonium, with her hoodie tied around her waist and her arms folded protectively across her chest. She bobbed her head to the racing rhythm. Studying her out of the corner of my eye, I adopted the same stance right next to her. I held tight to myself with one arm and used the other to shove people off me. We pushed in a bit closer and I started to catch the sweaty buzz. I drifted away from Jackie and closer to the stage. I hovered around the edges of the chaos, responding more enthusiastically to the jostles and shoves.

My brain soaked up the music until it felt like it had swelled too big for my skull, all its soft edges pushing up against a wall of bone. The speakers blew out my ears and I was gone, transported. I churned, trance-like in the spin-cycle of the crowd.

A few feet in front of me, a moshing skinhead took a hit that threw him off balance and he hurtled backwards. I saw his shiny pate flying straight at me, but didn't calculate an escape route quickly enough. When his head made contact with my jaw, I heard the thud as if it happened next to me or even further away. Blades of pain shot up into my head and down through my neck. Sparkly blackness closed in around my field of vision as I fell stiffly backward, barely clinging to consciousness. I tried to fight back from passing out, figuring I'd be trampled, but I couldn't catch myself. I hardly felt the impact by the time I hit the floor.

What seemed like a hundred hands lifted me up. The seemingly out-of-control crowd instantaneously parted to create an aisle through which I was carried out. I was weightless and safe and surrendered to unconsciousness.

When I came around a few minutes later I sat slumped against a wall out near the stairwell. The skinhead boy who knocked me out had propped me up and was holding a plastic cup of ice to my cheek. Other concerned faces I didn't know clustered behind him. He was bare-chested and dripping in sweat.

"Are you alright? I'm really sorry. Are you alright?" He asked with a deep wrinkle of concern between his heavy brows.

He was the cutest guy I had ever seen. He asked me over and over again if I was alright until my mouth could form the words to respond.

"I'm okay. Thanks," was all I could think of. It hurt to smile, but I smiled at him anyway when he helped me to my feet.

He hung around close to me when we went back inside, like he was being protective so I wouldn't get hurt again, or maybe just because he liked me, too. I was so proud of myself. My first hardcore show and I had already been knocked unconscious and probably fallen in love at the same time.

Between bands I lost track of him. I was hanging around in the lobby telling a wide-eyed Jackie my war story and looking around for the newly-found love of my life when some skinny guy with a weird shirt and a piano-key scarf cornered me. He asked me how old I was. I lied for some reason and said sixteen; he replied with something creepy like, "Sixteen. Lots of good songs about sixteen." I managed to weasel away from him, but never did find my skinhead savior again that night.

Jackie and Tara and I reconvened as the Dickies took the stage, the last band of the night. The singer was the piano key scarf guy.

"That lead singer came on to me in the lobby," I told Tara. "I thought he was just some sleazy guy."

"Maybe he is some sleazy guy," Tara laughed. "He just also happens to be the singer for the Dickies. Don't let it bum you out. Don't confuse the art with the artist. Go out and make your own art, Jill."

I was exhausted, my ears were ringing and my whole face throbbed with pain, but I still wished the night would go on longer. I wished I could live there forever. At least when I went home the next day, to the purgatory of the suburbs, I wouldn't feel as alone as I had before. The band played and I knew that even though this music was something wildly new and exciting, it had been in me all along.

WILD SURROGATES

Blake Schwarzenbach

In 1981 I had just moved to Los Angeles from Portland, Oregon, where I was to begin my secondary education at a semi-preparatory school, called Crossroads, in Santa Monica. Somehow, I had lucked into a copy of Echo and the Bunnymen's *Crocodiles* LP, a Wipers 7", and a Sado-Nation 7", before moving south. I understood nothing about these records except that they were scary and represented some forbidden adult world involving angry sex and nocturnal patterns. I was particularly fond of the Bunnymen jacket, the moribund characters languishing in the artificially lit forest. It reminded me of *Night of the Living Dead*, arguably the punkest movie ever made in America. The characters appeared startled and melancholy, waking to find themselves suddenly disenfranchised; but they also stood as a kind of loosely assembled mob, united by grief. Retaliation seemed imminent. This doomed sensibility resounded strongly in the Northwest—an area of perpetual night and rain, the bums and wayward Indians on Burnside, the old and crumbling world of industry, bridges, and trains going nowhere. Whatever understanding I had for this emerging culture was thoroughly zeroed by the fixed sun of LA.

My dad and I lived in a rented house in Venice, where I quickly made the acquaintance of my neighbor, Brendan Murdock. He came into my room one day while I was practicing the drums and introduced himself. A very vivid specimen—basically a lithe coil of muscle tightly encased in freckles. He told me that he also played drums and invited me over to his garage where he convinced me that I should immediately take up guitar because it was clear I would never play like he did. This was in the late summer, just before school. He was my only friend in the world. A cultural exchange ensued—skateboarding, arcading, bodysurfing, bus-taking. One night, he told me we were going to the Fox Theater in Venice to see something really crazy called *The Decline of Western Civilization*. The California truth: my first punk show was a movie.

Like any good punk show, getting there was half the fun. We had to walk from our relatively secure seaside sector at Pacific Street, across the no man's land called "Ghost Town," to the art house on Lincoln Boulevard, which we believed to be the next outpost of civilization. "Ghost Town" loomed large in the white imagination of the time—it was thought to be packed with bandits and V13 (our premier gang), motorcyclists and drug ranchers, mixed marriages, same-sex cohabitants, surrealists, fomented Marxists. Basically anything that we couldn't be or know lived there. The cinematic allegory that springs to mind is Mos Eisley port. More coarsely drawn, it was the repository for blacks and Mexicans on the west side of LA, a holdout colony, forfeited by white developers who feared to tread, a concession. Needless to say, we were psyched.

I remember little of the walk or even the film. We moved straight and fast, eyes forward, making up gibberish conversation when we met a group along the way, so as to appear occupied. There was, however, much to talk about on the way home. I wanted to be many characters in the film, or a composite of those I found winning, and I definitely wanted to play music. I wanted to live with Exene and have her read the Bible to me, but I wanted to sleep in Chavo's closet at the Black Flag church, under an American flag with cigarette burns in it. Lee Ving would be my uncle who would teach me about horse racing, and would let me drink one beer while we worked on his car. What was important about the film was that it suggested there was a place to go, even if the place it showed had already been condemned or evicted or had fled. Reagan was high atop his wave of white teeth and superman hair; a new techno-fascist architecture was sweeping the streets, with its mirrored cathedrals and gymnasiums; commercial music had left the audible realm, disappeared in wow and flutter, no lyrics or melodies, just electric drums and digital sheen. Yet, in spite of all this damning evidence, there was Eugene saying, "It's raw again and it's for real…and it's fun." *The Decline* heralded a new beginning, by destroying everything that was false and saying we do not need your help or patronage—this is our vacant lot, we have burned it back to earth and will do as we see fit. I don't know that any of this occurred to me at the time, it just seemed better than everything else that was going on. "Ghost Town" was actually the only hope for civilization. In the words of D. Boon (and I think the best lyrical summation of first-show giddiness): "We were fucking corn dogs."

A NIGHT AT THE ANTENNA CLUB, MEMPHIS

Ben Sizemore

It was 1984 and I was thirteen going on fourteen. My favorite bands were the Dead Kennedys, Black Flag, and Minor Threat. I was probably wearing a pair of Levis that I had ripped up and scrawled the name of every punk or quasi-punk band I had ever heard of on. From The Sex Pistols and The Clash, to Devo, to MDC, and The Feederz and every band on the *Let Them Eat Jellybeans* compilation—even the weird ones on the B-Side. I was trying to express my utter punkness, and quantity was paramount. Since I didn't know any better, maybe some new wave bands were written on them too, like U2 and The Police, who were my favorite bands before I got my first punk record: *Plastic Surgery Disasters* by the DK's. My buddy Mike Jackson gave it to me for my thirteenth birthday. I decided, instantly, that I wanted to be a punk when I heard that record.

I had always been into music; my older brother was a heavy metal drummer who took me to see Van Halen and Iron Maiden. Later I got into new wave. I "went with" a girl for a week from my jr. high whose favorite band was the B-52's. They were probably written in magic marker on those fucking ridiculous jeans, as well. I think I was also wearing a button-down army shirt decorated in the same manner as the jeans and some Chuck Taylors. I had a crew cut—but with a rattail, leftover from my parachute pants days. It was the '80s after all.

I had been desperately trying to get into the Antenna Club with my punk mentor and best friend, Mike, for months. It was the coolest place in Memphis, Tennessee and it was in Midtown, our neighborhood, just a few minutes bike ride from home.

We were hicks from somewhat redneck backgrounds. I was from Little Rock, Arkansas, but halfway through seventh grade, my parents moved us to Memphis. There I discovered punk culture and skateboarding—I often wonder what my life would have been like if I hadn't. Anyway, we'd seen flyers for the show on telephone poles around town. We must have told our parents we were going to a party, and it must not have been a school night, because I don't remember having to sneak out or lie excessively. The Antenna Club was the only place in over a hundred mile radius that would actually have real, live, touring punk bands play—but it was still a bar and we were kids. I wound up seeing loads of shows there, but I never really understood the policy they had on letting us in. (To this day I am still pissed off that I missed the Minutemen and Negative Approach shows that had happened earlier that year, so gaining entry to this gig was the most important thing in the world to me at the time.) When Black Flag played we couldn't get in and had to sit outside and listen through the side door because it was over-twenty-one, but other nights when it wasn't so crowded, or maybe when Rebel, the biker-bouncer, wasn't at the door, they'd let us in. Sometimes I used this incredibly cheesy fake ID to get in. My name on it was "Ben Saccharin." It was so corny!

On this particular evening we were determined to see the show. It was going to be my first punk show and probably Mike's as well, although he was way too cool to admit it. I can't remember exactly how it worked, but we just walked in, plunked down our $5, and got our hands stamped. Later I would sneak into The Necros show by hiding in a bass drum case, but luckily such drastic measures weren't necessary on this night. Once beyond the threshold, we quickly walked to a corner table up front and hunkered down, knowing we weren't supposed to be there.

The place was a very dark, low, rectangular-shaped room; it reeked of stale smoke and beer. There were probably about forty people there and most didn't give a fuck about hardcore. They were there for the cheap alcohol. The crowd consisted of local rednecks, new wavers, jarheads from the marine base, and a few druggie-types in trench coats. Then there was us: about fifteen under-age kids into punk, hardcore, and skateboarding. Mike and me were the only ones from Midtown; the other kids were mostly from Germantown, a rich suburb. We didn't know them yet, but we sat by them.

Mike had no fear. He started a conversation with Andy Campora, a jovial guy with a flattop and a JFA shirt on. He was twenty-one, actually old enough to be there, and had a job and his own apartment near the club. After deciding we weren't posers he accepted us as fellow punkers. Andy instantly became the coolest person we had ever met and we could prove to him that we had some knowledge since we'd been reading *MRR* and *Flipside*, and listening to punk for nearly a year. Luckily for us, Memphis had Rare Records, a little shop in our neighborhood that carried punk records and zines along with college rock stuff like REM. (We went there once to see Henry Rollins read from his first poetry book, but that was later.)

Andy introduced us to his younger brother and sister, who were also into punk and skateboarding. We also met his buddy Dan—a seriously pissed off looking kid with a shaved head, who had once run away from home to LA—and all their other pals. Needless to say, they were almost all teenage white dudes. There were only a few girls in the group and, of course, I instantly formed crushes on them all. By the time the first band came on we had actually made some friends with kids like us! We quickly bonded over being punks in the Bible Belt. It was easy since we felt oppressed daily by rednecks, jocks, our parents, cops, teachers, and basically everyone, just for looking different. People called us faggots and tried to beat us up. There were about a million people in the Memphis area, but only a handful of us. This both sucked and made us proud.

The opening band was a Germantown outfit, Mad Rats. They mostly played covers of Black Flag and the Circle Jerks. The pit erupted halfway through the first song with Andy and Dan leading the charge. The dance floor extended out from the stage about fifteen feet, and the kids were going back and forth across it thrashing and then resting against the wall between songs. I was too chicken to enter at first. It looked pretty rough and reminded me of a football game, but when Mike entered, during the "Jealous Again" cover, I had to join. I half ran and half skipped, back and forth smashing into the others with all my might so they wouldn't think I was a wimp. At one point someone did a stage-dive but landed on their feet since there weren't enough people to do a real one. The set was a blur. Being there and thrashing was an insane rush that left me breathless, but once they left the stage I was dying for more. I was instantly hooked and knew I had to see every punk band there was immediately. I felt high, but I'd had no drugs or alcohol.

The second band was the Stretch Marks from Canada. We had heard them on the BYO Records compilation *Something to Believe In* and knew they were rad. I remember their singer had a short spiked hair and was wearing a colorful Hawaiian shirt. He came out and announced whom they were and where they were from. The guitarist hit the first chord, the whole band leapt into the air, and the pit erupted simultaneously. I think I got an elbow in the chin and bit into my tongue. My mouth filled with blood, but so what? I couldn't feel the pain and it looked cool when I spit blood on the floor. It was like the Target punk videos me and Mike had watched dozens of times, and we tried to mimic the moves we'd seen there in the pit.

The set went at blazing speed, but these guys were louder, faster, and more intense than the Mad Rats, and I couldn't believe they were right there: you could reach out and touch them. It was nothing like seeing Billy Squire at Barton Coliseum, which was probably my first rock concert. These guys weren't rock stars. They looked you in the eye and pushed the mic in your face to let you scream along. You felt like you were part of making the show happen. You felt like you were part of the music and it felt fucking urgent.

Back then, we thought Reagan was going to start a nuclear war with the USSR and that the world was gonna end unless we did something about it! I thought punks were going to lead the way and start a revolution. It was gonna be like the cover of Youth Brigade's *Sound and Fury* album goddamnit! I was completely fuckin blown away by the Stretch Marks. Mike bought the record and I got a t-shirt for a grand total of $10 and we made small talk with their roadie.

Channel 3, from southern California, were the headliners. We had their *Fear of Life* record, which was on the famous Posh Boy label. "Separate Peace" and "Mannequin" were my favorites songs of theirs, and as they set up I began plotting my thrash moves for when they played. The record they were touring to support was *Airborne* and it looked kind of lame. They had big hair, but not charged like GBH or Discharge—instead it looked more like the hairdos from the guys in The Alarm. Basically they looked like glam dudes in black with some studded belts. Still, I liked them, and when they played the songs I knew, I went nuts.

The show was so fucking intense and compelling, it's no wonder I've probably been to a thousand since. I felt free. All my problems melted away. I didn't feel alone. I didn't feel like a complete dork, even though I must have looked and acted like one. I could release all the pent up anger I felt inside about my life, my surroundings, and of course about my alcoholic dad. The punk kids me and Mike met that night accepted us immediately and we would become part of the scene. Later, we'd put on our own all-ages shows; we'd do *Bullsheet* fanzine together; we'd become straight edge and I would actually remain that way; we'd get more into leftist politics and read more; we'd start bands. I would have to move back to Little Rock, but I'd make punk friends there and my band Econochrist would actually play our first show back at the Antenna Club! We'd base our lives on punk culture: the music, the lyrics, the fashion, the politics, and the lifestyle. For a long time punk/hardcore would be, by far, the most important thing in our lives.

Looking back on it all, I've lost touch with all those guys from that first show. Mike is still real into music but mostly industrial and experimental stuff the last I heard, and that was over ten years ago. Andy and his siblings were from a Christian family, and I guess punk was just a phase for them after all. They were "born again" and became missionaries. I heard Dan came out of the closet and quit going to punk shows. Not sure about the other folks there that night, maybe I should look them up on Myspace. For a few years, back then in Memphis, we were family and our lives were changed profoundly and permanently by punk rock.

That first show for me was the hook. Now I'm thirty-five and I still go to punk shows and listen to hardcore, but it's not all that I'm into. I still consider myself a punk, but I can't shake the feeling that the best years of my life have happened, and that the feelings I had back then will never be repeated.

PASADENA, 1983

Jamie Reilly

My first time was a false start. It was 1983 and I was thirteen. GBH was playing at Perkins Palace in Pasadena, where I lived. I didn't love GBH (but like all good skaters, I had the requisite "Charged GBH" sticker on my skateboard); I wanted to go because Social Distortion was opening, and after putting out a few 45s—all of which I had taped from my friend's older sister—they had just released *Mommy's Little Monster,* their first full length record, which was spectacular. I thought they were the bee's knees.

I had tried to go to other punk shows with friends, but the big shows at the time were at the Olympic Auditorium, in downtown LA. It was an area my parents didn't feel safe driving through, so they always rejected my proposals without negotiation. I had convinced my dad to let me go to the GBH show, in large part because it was local, and with the one stipulation that I bring someone older with me. Luckily, I was friends with a girl named Christina who was a year older than me, but two grades ahead. She was into cool music, but most importantly, her dad was a math teacher at our school, giving her near legal guardian status with my parents. I also had a huge crush on her, so in my mind, when she said she would go to the show with me, it was not only going to be my first concert, it was going to be my first date. What could be better?

As the end of the week approached, my pragmatic father suggested we pick up the tickets from the box office the day before, so my date wouldn't be spoiled by a possible sell-out. Great idea! So Friday night he whisked me down to Perkins Palace in our pale yellow Buick. As he pulled up to the box office I gulped. There was a show that night too: Alien Sex Fiend. Fuck. A whole line of death rockers in black veils and black fingernails swiveled to look at the baby faced punk getting out of Daddy's car. Sweet. I got in line and looked around while my dad waited in the car, looking—for the first time in his life—at heterosexual men in makeup. I think he might have waved to me. God, it was tough being an adolescent. When my turn came, I explained to the girl at the box office that, in fact, I wanted two tickets to the show the following evening. I handed her two weeks dog walking money and she handed me the tickets. I got back in the car and we headed home. "Were you scared?" my dad asked me. "No," I scoffed. I know I was thirteen, but I was already pushing 6 feet, and punk was still pretty foreign to most suburbanites. When people saw me on the bus, they didn't smile and they didn't sit near me. I figured the world was at least a little bit afraid of me. The truth of the matter was that those death rockers, with their fishnets and spider web makeup, had kind of weirded me out. But whatever, I had my tickets and those people wouldn't be at the show tomorrow. It was going to be all punk rockers, just like me.

I spent some time that night, before I went to bed, figuring out what I was going to wear the next day, which was a pretty simple process. I had one pair of sneakers, red Chuck Taylor high tops; two silk-screened shirts, Dead Kennedys "Holiday In Cambodia" and Sex Pistols "God Save the Queen," and two of my dad's old navy blue t-shirts that my mom had spilled bleach on; I had one pair of jeans that I had really put a lot of work into, writing the names of every band I liked, in as close an approximation of their logos as I could muster. And I would probably wear my flannel shirt with the George Orwell quote sewn on the back. If I got too hot, I could always tie it around my waist.

The next day around lunchtime I called Christina; I was looking at the two tickets as the phone rang. "What time do you want to go tonight?" I asked. "Doors open at six. I think the first band goes on at seven, and there are five bands playing. Do you want to get something to eat first or just go straight there?" When I finished talking she was quiet for a second. She said, "I'm grounded right now. I can't go out."

Fuck. Fuck. Fuck. Fuck. Fuck. Fuck. Fuck. Fuck. Fuck. Fuck. Fuck. Fuck. Fuck. Fuck.

Act nonchalant.

"Bummer." Shit. Shit. Shit. Shit. Shit. Shit. Shit. Shit. "You think you could sneak out?"

"No. I have to stay here," she said. "I'll see you at school on Monday. Tell me all about it."

"You bet. So long." Fuck. Shit.

Oh man, this sucked. An emotional blow, and also a financial set back. In hindsight, I guess I could have gone to the show to sell the tickets. I spent the rest of the day trying to think of someone else who could take me. I came up blank. I ate the cost of the tickets, and spent the next month or so trying to convince my parents to let me go to shows with one of my friends my own age.

After a lot of work, I succeeded. I got the ok to go to a show with my best friend Joe Nollar. We had known each other for ten years, our families were friends, and I spent almost all my free time with him. The only problem was that he didn't really like punk. He tolerated it, but he was into Ska. I figured I could get him to come along when the chance arose. He'd probably even pay his own way.

The next big show at Perkins Palace was a BYO show in conjunction with the release of their record *Something to Believe In*. I think it was the early part of 1984. I was either thirteen or had just turned fourteen. I went; Joe came along. My mom dropped us off and picked us up. (A block away from the show so we could walk up to the door without it *looking* like my mom had dropped us off.) I can't remember if all the bands on the record played, but I am pretty sure most of them did.

We got there late and we had to leave early. We missed 7 Seconds (who I would see over and over again in the summers that followed) and Youth Brigade (who I would never get to see), SNFU, and some other bands I didn't care about.

I remember a few things about the show in particular. Rigor Mortis was playing when we got in. The singer had his hair short on the sides and on the top was a foot-high spike pointing straight up—sort of a Kid n' Play precursor. I didn't think their music was that great, but the venue sure was. Perkins was a big old movie theater, so there was an actual (orchestra) pit in front of where the slam circle was.

I remember a kid with a double mohawk and a Minor Threat shirt on. I loved Minor Threat, whose record I had bought based largely on their photos in Glen Friedman's *My Rules* magazine—I didn't drink so I immediately thought of Glen as a friend. The kid went apeshit during the show, doing stage-dives and getting chased by bouncers. I later saw him knocking back beers outside.

The singer of the next band came out and said "We're Stretch Marks, from Winnipeg, Canada." Whenever anyone says "Winnipeg," to this day, I silently repeat that phrase in my head. During their set, when Joe and I were standing in the orchestra pit, someone did a flip off the stage and hit me in the head with an army boot. Feeling dizzy, I sat down.

After about fifteen minutes, a girl walked up and began asking me some question over and over, but I couldn't fully understand because of the noise. Finally, it came through clearly: "Do you have any Fry?" Oh. Now that I heard the question, I was sure I didn't understand it. What was Fry? Best to take the straightforward approach.

"What is Fry?" I asked her.

"Acid. I heard you had Acid."

"Ohhhhhhhh. Nope." Sure didn't. That was for hippies. And, uh, I'm only a little kid. Do I look like the go-to guy for your fix? My forehead is covered with pimples and it's only by the grace of God I don't have headgear on.

I guess she was pissed off that it had taken so long to get a "no" out of me; she rolled her eyes and stomped off. Oh well. Stretch Marks were done and the next band was setting up. My mom was going to be back to pick us up in forty-five minutes, so I prayed they would be good.

As they came out, my heart dropped: they were longhairs, and they had on goofy jewelry. The lead singer/guitar player stepped up to the mic, "We're Channel 3, from Cerritos!" WTF? I had a few CH3 songs on some compilations, like "Catholic Boy" and "You Make Me Feel Cheap," but they were hard. These guys were dressed like Van Halen! The songs they were singing were stinkers; the one I remember most clearly was called "Indian Summer." I think there may have been some booing/ice throwing from the crowd.

There was a saving grace however: they played some of their older songs. "Manzanar," "I've Got A Gun," and "Catholic Boy" made the place go wild. But it was time for us to go. We were going to meet my mom at the Espresso Bar so she could drive us home. As we walked, Joe told me he thought C-H-3 was pretty good. "Channel 3," I said. "I like to say it C-H-3," he told me.

My mom was having coffee at the E bar and asked us how it was. I guess it was pretty good. By far the best part about it was that it popped my cherry. Since I didn't get beat up or die or join the Moonies, it increased the chances that I would be able to go to other shows in the future. The "Something To Believe In" show was, it seemed, the end of an era. The big punk bands of the early-80s had played in a lot of big marquee venues; Black Flag even played the Santa Monica Civic Center. It seemed that sort of thing happened less and less often.

By the end of 1984, I had made friends with a couple older punk kids and I started going to shows with them every weekend. That was really a far more influential era for me, '84–88: I was in high school, and there were tons of new bands in Southern California, although it meant smaller scenes and smaller shows. The shows were utilitarian, not hugely promoted events. It was usually eight bands/$8. I don't think I went to another show in a venue the size of Perkins Palace for the rest of the '80s.

REVIVAL

Jesse Pires

My father had an unusual way of saying "no" when I was a kid. If I wanted money or permission, or if I wanted to deviate from his fatherly authority, he would rarely say "no." Instead, he would say, "let me think about it." This, I quickly learned, was his great delaying tactic—if he could circumvent the question long enough I would ultimately forget and move on to something else. But my dad is also an amazingly smart and cool guy with great taste in music. In his lifetime, he's seen the Velvet Underground, Sun Ra, and Fela Kuti. So when it came time to go to my first hardcore show, I assumed he would have been a bit more understanding.

In the early spring of 1989, hardcore pioneers Bad Brains were on tour—albeit without their legendary lead singer, HR. They were playing a show at Revival in Philadelphia, a forty-five minute train ride away from my suburban wasteland. My friends, who had been taking the R5 to see hardcore shows for several months, were busy gearing up for the Bad Brains. For the past year, I had been taking the same train into the city to attend Saturday art classes at Moore College of Art. Naturally, I assumed there was no reason for my dad to keep me from going.

I was just weeks away from my fifteenth birthday; I pressed him to let me go. He gave me the perfunctory "let me think about it." But this time his method didn't work. After continued pestering he was finally forced to say no, but he said—inexplicably—that I would be allowed to go next time. I suspect he didn't realize that there was a hardcore matinee in Philadelphia just about every weekend. And, lo and behold, there was another one several weeks later. Though not as pioneering or legendary as Bad Brains, Adrenalin O.D. was still a pretty kick-ass band, a good choice for my first show.

Donning my 7 Seconds "Walk Together, Rock Together" shirt, cut-off army fatigues, and a chain with a padlock around my neck, I ventured into the city with my friends Jeremy and Dean. I possessed equal amounts of youthful enthusiasm and trepidation. The building that housed Revival was a neo-classical structure—complete with towering columns—located in the heart of Philadelphia's Old City district. It was just a block away from 3rd Street Records, an amazing store that my father and I both frequented before it closed its doors in the late-90s.

From the outside, Revival looked like a church. Inside, however, it was the quintessential punk club. There was a bar on one side with TV monitors playing the infamous video of Budd Dwyer's public suicide over and over again. There were a couple of orange vinyl couches on the other side. Scattered throughout the dystopian landscape were about 100 or so kids wandering around, waiting for the next band to go on. It was like that scene in *Repo Man* when they go to the club and the Circle Jerks are playing "When the Shit Hits the Fan," only with a bit more Philly attitude.

I honestly can't say that I remember who the first band was. It could have been Scab Cadillac, Uptown Bones, The Big Thing, or Dead Spot—all of whom I would end up seeing at Revival in the year to come. We lingered in the back, perusing the merch table for the first set. Next on stage was the Pagan Babies, a band that would completely transform my interpretation of punk rock. We moved up front to get a better look. The lead singer, clad in a Flyers Jersey, was ferocious and brash and the band was tight and heavy. This was also the golden era of the second wave of hip-hop (Boogie Down Productions, Public Enemy) and this band was a fantastic fusion of urban hip-hop style and punk rock attitude. The drummer looked like he could've been a Beastie Boy, while the guitarists were pure South Philly. As I stood there, off to the side, with my friend Jeremy behind me, I thought to myself, "This is definitely where I belong."

A couple songs into the Pagan Babies set, a few kids in front of the stage started to mosh. As a few others joined in, someone was thrown into me. "This is it," I thought, "I'm going to get the shit beat out of me and my parents are going to be so pissed." I turned back to my friend Jeremy, who smiled reassuringly and nodded. I soon realized that part of the punk show experience was not only watching the band but also watching the violent spectacle of the slam-dancers and moshers. All of that would, of course, be called into question later that summer at the Frankford YMCA when I got to see Fugazi for the first time.

The only real drama of the day unfolded between sets; I was standing alone at the rear of the club when a guy a few years older than me approached. "Hey man, you got a dollar?" he asked.

My naïve, suburban, fifteen-year-old self came bubbling back up to the surface. "Here's a five...that's all I have, take it," I said.

I immediately felt like the biggest schmuck in the room.

I can only hope that this guy, who probably wanted to get a bottle of water, was so thrilled by my generosity that he tipped the bartender an extra couple bucks. Somehow, I doubt that happened though.

Shortly before A.O.D. went on, another guy came up to me. "Did you just give my brother five dollars?" he said.

I smiled and nodded as I could feel the nervous sweat building under my padlock and chain. The guy just shook his head and walked away. I had made the trek to the big city to my first hardcore show just to find out what a poser I really was. I shrug it off now, but at the time it really felt like my cover was blown.

A.O.D. finally took the stage and started with the riff-heavy "A.O.D. vs. Godzilla." I have to admit that the rest of the set was not as memorable or as mind-blowing as I'd hoped. This was shortly after their *Cruisin' with Elvis in Bigfoot's UFO* release, and all I could think was, "These guys kinda look like old hippies." After the show, ears ringing, we all boarded the R5 train back to Lansdale. That year I would end up attending dozens of hardcore shows, singing in a hardcore band, starting a fanzine, and finally getting to see Bad Brains—with HR—at Revival. He might not admit it, but I have a feeling my dad was pretty proud.

PUNK ROCK, WHERE ASSHOLES STILL WANT EVERYTHING FOR FREE!

Blag Dahlia

My first punk show was the Angelic Upstarts in Chicago. This was when the Metro was called Stages and employed an army of Mr. T-like bouncers. It was an all-ages show, but I didn't bring an ID, so they wouldn't let me or my friend in. We hung out on the sidewalk smoking brown pot and drinking malt liquor instead.

I had my long hair tied into a series of ridiculous looking braids all over my head, like a pubescent Pippi Longstocking: this was because I'd heard that hippies were unacceptable to punks and I didn't want to stick out.

I started talking to a girl I met outside the liquor store. She had a haircut that looked like a comma balanced on her head and a drunken scowl on her face. When her older boyfriend came out of the liquor store he told me to fuck off with a mouth that smelled like old carpeting moldering in a dumpster. I said fuck you and a standoff ensued. They went into the show and I planned my next move—more drinking.

Within the next couple of years I saw The Replacements, Hüsker Dü, Black Flag, Minor Threat, MDC, Dead Kennedys, the Cramps, Ramones, Gang of Four, and many more, but I never forgot that scowling girl and her retarded boyfriend. I still see them at every punk show I go to. That's why I don't go to them anymore unless I'm getting paid!

MY FIRST TIME: A HEARTWARMING TALE

Anna Brown

Eighth grade was a rough year for me. I started growing apart from all my grade school friends. Kids I had been tight with since third grade suddenly seemed shallow and ridiculous to me. A great specter of gloom settled over me and colored my views about everything. My friends noticed too, and eventually quit including me in things. I ate lunch by myself and lost interest in all the junior high school things I should have been enjoying, like dances and parties. When summer finally came and all the neighborhood kids took off to tennis camp and Outward Bound, I found myself with nothing to do but read. My mom was studying for the California Bar Exam, and even holed up in my room reading S.E. Hinton or Ray Bradbury, I could feel tension all through the house. So I started spending most days on Telegraph Avenue in Berkeley with a loose-knit bunch of outcasts who hung out on the campus steps. I would leave the house in the morning with my camera and a couple dollars worth of babysitting money—if I was lucky—and trek the two miles north to the Berkeley campus, stopping by Slash, the basement thrift store, on the way to flirt pathetically with the cute mod guy who sold me my t-shirts and army jackets.

I could usually count on running into Kim, Marsha, Clawed, Dave Half-Head, Lint, Little Joe, those two skinhead brothers from Long Beach, Joe Dread, or a dozen other kids with nothing to do but maybe some table-diving at La Val's. Sometimes we would see if we could get onto the roofs of the campus buildings and dorms, drink coffee at the Med, or just sit on Sproul Plaza, waiting for something to happen, always to the soundtrack of standards provided by Rick Starr and his tiny PA system.

I had smoked pot before with my school friends—growing up in Berkeley everyone's parents had a stash that was pretty accessible to their kids—but that was the only experimenting I had ever done with drugs. So when Alexandra offered me a hit of acid one afternoon I said "sure." After all, I wanted to know about everything, and what did I know about acid? Besides having read *That was Then This is Now* where M&M thinks spiders are crawling all over him, and *Go Ask Alice*, where she dies in the end, all I knew was that it kind of felt like that egg in the frying pan in those "this is your brain on drugs" ads. (At least according to Esther, the girl with the glass eye. "That's why they call it frying," she explained.) Alexandra charged me $1.00 for splitting a hit with her. She handed me a tiny piece of paper in the UC bathroom and instructed me to put it under my tongue and just keep it there. We sat on the steps watching the sun go down and gradually I started feeling it: my blood felt like it was carbonated and my mouth tasted like batteries. I knew I couldn't go home like this, so when all the kids from the steps announced they were heading down to Gilman I decided to go too. Gilman was a new punk club in a warehouse that had been having shows for a couple months. I heard people talking about it, but had never been there myself. When I walked into the dark warehouse and saw all the kids I recognized from around town and took in the electric walls covered with murals and graffiti, I was in awe. Where were the grown-ups and the asshole tough guys? Why hadn't I been here before?

This was the alternate universe where everyone went at night to smoke cigarettes, flail around to the bands playing their hearts out, guzzle coffee, and plot the revolution. I was transfixed watching an older guy, maybe nineteen, shooting baskets into a hoop in the corner, and I watched him for what seemed like hours. When he passed me the ball and motioned for me to take a shot, it was like an invitation to join in the whole scene. He might as well have said "Gabba gabba hey, take a shot." The way I remember it, I was the world's most coordinated basket shooter, and I could not miss. The drugs were doing their thing now, and I felt in tune for the first time in months. Don't get me wrong, I felt crazy too. The faces of everyone around me looked slightly deformed; the writing on the walls writhed and undulated, the meaning of the words indecipherable; my own hands looked like they belonged to an alien creature. But even with the half-inflated red rubber ball we were using instead of a real basketball, I was swishing free throws one after another. The ball would trail orange light as it arced off my fingertips and found its way over and over into the hoop. The bands were loud and fast, and more exciting than anything I had ever seen.

The next morning my ears were ringing, I smelled like cigarettes, and I wanted more. Not more drugs, but more of the feeling that I was in the right place for once in my life. No one there expected me to look a certain way, to be happy or well adjusted. You weren't supposed to be happy. Fucking Multi Death corporations ruled the planet; there were CIA-sponsored wars in El Salvador; animals suffered at the hands of factory farm butchers!!! There was nothing wrong with me that wasn't wrong with all of us. Everyone's parents were a drag and school sucked, but it was cool cause when you got to the punk show none of that stuff mattered. It wasn't our fault we were pissed off—it was practically our duty. After all, I learned, society made us this way.

I started volunteering at the door, staying to clean up the club after the bands played, and eating donuts with the punks at Winchell's late into the night. The punks were smart and surprisingly well-organized. They managed to take everything and nothing seriously at the same time. It was like: "I'm okay, you're okay; it's the world that's fucked."

I was hooked. I spent the summer there, and the next ten years after that. I started bringing my younger sister along to shows when she turned twelve. Now I take my young cousins from suburban Arizona to Gilman when they visit, hoping they feel the same pull that I still do to the scene.

ADOLESCENTS AT GILMAN STREET, 1987

Russ Rankin

I had been to see a few bands before, mostly up at UCSC (University of California at Santa Cruz), but I was so drunk I really couldn't tell you their names (although I think one was called Vomit Launch so there's that...) or what they sounded like. Either way, I don't count them as "real" shows. I had also been to parties where bands happened to be playing, but again, I was there primarily to get fucked up, so the bands were incidental and I have only a shadowy recollection of these events.

My first legitimate foray into the world of punk shows was sometime in November or December of 1987 and it went down like this: A group of my friends had decided to rent a car and drive the hour and change up Highway 880 to Berkeley for a show. The venue was Gilman Street, and at that time it was still called the Gilman Street "Project" as it was being operated under the auspices of *Maximum RocknRoll* magazine. The headliners were the Adolescents—a band I was very excited to see (I had them painted down the right sleeve of my leather jacket!). We gathered the crew (about seven people crammed into a tiny vehicle), a bunch of liquor, and headed north.

It was a cold, but clear night as we found an empty church parking lot a few blocks away from the club. This was before the city of Berkeley had made its concerted efforts to gentrify the area, and Gilman Street was pretty deserted at night. Being newly sober I waited around in the cold while my friends pounded a case of beer in the vacant lot. I was giddy with nervous excitement—my first show! Finally the others were sufficiently buzzed and we headed up to the club.

The line wasn't huge and we were soon inside. We paid the requisite membership fee—I can't remember how much it was. I want to say it was a one-time charge of $2 and you got a year long membership (whereby you promised not to bring in any alcohol or drugs, start fights, or otherwise vandalize the place) and the shows themselves cost $5 for five bands. We cruised in and I was struck first of all with how small it seemed. There was graffiti all over the walls and ceiling and a basketball hoop on the wall to the right when you walked in, between the men's and women's bathrooms. The stage was in the far left corner, about two feet off the ground, and the bands' equipment was stacked over to the right. The crowd was mostly punk, leather jackets, bondage or bullet belts, doc martens, and spiky, dyed hair. I remember the blond girl working the door was named Honey (and was later featured in the Mr. T Experience song "Gilman Street"), and there were a few people who wore t-shirts that said "security," but other than that they looked liked everyone else. I later learned that everyone who "worked" at Gilman Street was a volunteer. The place was full, but not packed, and we found a place to stand and watch as the show started.

The first band was called Defiant Youth, and all I remember is that they had a big can of protein powder on stage. They said something about how it was the protein powder that the singer of the Slambodians used. After they were done, a band called Positive Outlook played some acceptable 'core. It was the era where straight edge was cool, and consequently, even bands that were nowhere near being drug-free used a lot of S.E. imagery and sang "positive" lyrics. I don't know if Positive Outlook was straight edge or not but they played a good set.

Next up was Hell's Kitchen, who I think were from across the bay in San Francisco, and they looked like big fat bikers. They had two guitars and were extremely loud. The music was pretty metal in a way that reminded me of bands like Fang or Tales of Terror; that is to say that they weren't exactly "metal" per se, but that they had a lot of the trappings of that genre. Their set was good—at one point the singer got up onto one of the big fat guitarist's shoulders, which I thought was cool. The main support band was San Jose's Frontline and they were awesome. I had the pleasure of seeing them several times after this. (They changed their name to Lifeline for a while, then broke up. Their singer Joe "Sib" Subbiondo went on to front Wax, 22 Jacks, and is now running Side One Dummy records.) Their great melodies and Joe's natural and endearing stage presence made that night's set a memorable one. Between songs he was talking up the Adolescents, and it was clear they were friends.

I was getting more and more excited. Though there had been a pretty healthy circle pit the whole show, I had stayed in the back. I knew I wanted to go into a "real" pit, but I was reluctant at the same time. My heart was beating out of my chest and I was incredibly restless as the Adolescents set up their gear.

It was an interesting time in the life of the Adolescents. Original singer Tony Cadena had left to front The Flower Leperds, and original drummer Casey Royer was now singing for D.I. full-time. The vocal duties were now being split by bassist Steve Soto and guitarist Rikk Agnew. Rounding out this edition of the legendary band was Sandy Hansen on drums and another guitar player, whose name escapes me (but it wasn't Frank Agnew—I know that). This is the line-up that appeared on the 1988 release *Balboa Fun Zone*, which, from an Adolescents fan's perspective, is either quirky and fun or utterly forgettable, depending on your point of view.

I don't remember what they opened with, nor can I recall the subtleties of the extensive set list. I remember not being bothered by the fact that all these familiar songs were being sung by someone other than Tony. I remember the band's "stage" guy, Steve "Ace" Acevedo, throwing people off the stage whenever they tried to come up and share the mic with Rikk. The pit was going now and there were people diving off of either side of the stage. The entire floor of the club seemed to be a swirling mass of leather and flannel. I stood on the edge of the pit, heart pumping, as I sang along to every line. At one point (I think it was during the bass refrain of "Do the Freddy"), I remember Rikk tossing his guitar off and jumping into the pit (which I found utterly shocking)! Then finally, as the opening guitars of "Wrecking Crew" plunked off the graffiti-caked walls, one of my friends grabbed me, threw his arm over my shoulder and shoved us both into the pit. There was no turning back now! As the mellow, yet haunting intro stopped and Rikk shouted: "We're just a wrecking crew, bored boys with nothing to do!" the entire floor seemingly erupted and I was swept up into it. My friend and I tromped around the circle, pinwheeling left and right, fists pumping in the air as we bounced off the people who stood on the edges of the dance floor. They pushed and shoved us back in when we stumbled too close. It was electric—I swear I didn't come down from it for hours, and I remember being grateful that I was able to experience it sober.

As we were filing out of the club, I remember Rikk Agnew standing by the door shaking everybody's hands, and when he shook mine, I was struck with how awesome punk rock was, and how there really didn't have to be any rock stars or separation between the bands and the audience. It was a special night for me and the beginning of a lengthy love affair with the little club on Gilman Street. Over the next three years I would find myself there almost every weekend, even staying late to help sweep up after the show a few times. I saw Green Day there when they were still called Sweet Children, I saw NOFX, Bad Religion, and The Offspring there before they became hugely popular, and to a greater degree, I learned a lot about community and unity. Countless times, I saw fights or confrontations handled from within by concerned members of the Gilman Street "scene," who knew that their precious venue could easily be taken away from them if they didn't police themselves. I saw shows stop when disrupted by racists or BASH (Bay Area Skinheads) and the agitators surrounded, outnumbered, and shown the door. Seldom did it devolve into violence. The monthly membership meetings (which I never attended, but always meant to), as well as the monthly record swaps... it was all part of a utopian piece of punk history that I feel happy to have experienced. For a few magical years the Gilman Street Project personified the promise of punk rock and how a community of aware, like-minded people were able to create a place where a counter culture blossomed; where bands and audience became one. It was a place I will never forget.

THE TURNING POINT

Harrison Haynes

There used to be this place...I'm not sure what happened to it, but I'm surprised more people don't discuss its significant contribution to Chapel Hill's musical/cultural legacy.

It was an inconspicuous industrial space behind Sparkle Car Wash, known as The Turning Point. The main room had a garage door that could be opened onto the street and another room served as the everyday entrance. A smaller boxed-in room had a lowered ceiling and a lofted attic above it, but the main ceiling was a tall half-arch spanned by exposed rafters, making you feel like you were in a barn.

A family lived in there: Brian, a dour British hippy; a woman (his wife?), whose name and face I can't remember; and a quiet kid my age (their son, I think), named Ezra. Despite all my curiosity about this unusual situation, I don't remember ever asking, "so, what's the deal with these people?" What *was* the deal with those people?

As well as being home to that odd clan, The Turning Point was also
a place where bands played. That is how I came to know about it. This
all took place between 1986–87 in Carrboro and Chapel Hill, North
Carolina. A small group of us sycophantic early-teens would hear about
a show and walk the mile and a half or so from Uptown Chapel Hill—
from the Post Office, from the Church Steps, from Barrel of Fun, or from
Sadlack's—to The Turning Point to check it out, certain that it would be
cool no matter what.

The shows were in the late afternoons or early evenings on weekends. Sometimes, before the show we would get invited (actually more
of an unspoken agreement reliant on the nervy action of following a
group into the undergrowth) to sit in the woods near a graveyard to
drink cans of warm beer, feigning apathy while scrutinizing the gestures
and language of the older kids. I must have sounded ridiculous, chiming in
with an occasional "yeah, man," since my voice was still very high.

The scene was probably similar to things going on in many other
small towns around that time: a range of introverts gathering on the
streets at night to hang out and emulate their perception of underground culture and music. Some of the looks and attitudes going on
were unique hybrids, and others were just attempts at a creative rebellion (I'll use "punk rock" here for lack of anything more articulate). But
for us aspiring young punks, each denizen—no matter how impossible to
classify—was an icon. We referred to them by name as you might refer
to a celebrity: "Andy Roberts ate some mushrooms" or "Chris Blake
was Uptown last night."

The first show I went to at The Turning Point was in the summertime.
The lineup was Corrosion of Conformity, Resist, and Fist of Fury. The atmosphere was chaotic, and by that I just mean messy and uncertain. The
garage door was open while the bands played, and people were standing
around inside and on the street in front. The stage was a low, shoddy
platform at the back of the space and there was junk piled up around
it: a skeletal couch, boxes, destroyed sculptures, and piles of clothes.
There was more junk piled up in the attic space atop the small room,
and someone was referring to that area, saying, "Yeah…Dennis fucked
Teddy up there." This disturbed me because Teddy was a cool older girl
I had a crush on, and Dennis was a delinquent bully. I never found out if
the statement was factual. Later on, maybe a year later, Teddy signed my
yearbook with the crushing line: "Call when you grow tall."

Despite the undeniable role this event played in my becoming a musician, the details of it in my memory are entirely visual. I noticed that C.O.C.'s singer/bass player looked like a wino with droopy sweatpants and matted hair, and that he wore an old backpack while he played. I remember Resist's guitarist, a thickset dude in densely studded leather jacket and liberty spikes, because I thought he could probably smash through a brick wall. I remember this pink-faced guy called Wolf. He and a handful of other Fort Bragg enlistees (The Rats) would come up to the shows to drink Busch and get violent. I can picture him stumbling around in the audience, sweaty, in big, loose motorcycle boots.

The whole assembly felt surprisingly insubstantial and crappy compared with my glorified expectations of what a punk rock show would be. And it wasn't until I started going to see bands at the Brewery (a typical rock club with a PA and a stage) that I was able to grasp how singularly weird The Turning Point was.

Lately, I'm only able to find a few people who remember it at all.

CLENCHED FISTS, OPEN EYES: MY FIRST PUNK SHOW

Joseph A. Gervasi

I stood in the center of a whirlwind. Around me the pimpled titans clashed. Testosterone, hair dye, studs, and sick boys fucked angst in a North Philly disco club blender.

I was the skinny one in the cut-off denim shorts and a t-shirt for the band I had hoped to see, 7 Seconds. I was sporting the most rebellious haircut my parents would let me adopt: the mullet. This was not the ironic mullet that one is likely to see nowadays. Irony was still a few years away in the fad-regurgitating '90s. No, friends, this was July 1987 and the dubious 'do was the most noble effort I could make in expressing my burgeoning love affair with psychedelic, speed metal, and—we are gathered here today—hardcore punk rock.

From the moment I entered Club Pizazz and saw the turmoil of "da pit," I was struck by one life defining thought: *I fucked up.*

***

Let's first slip the slide under the microscope and look back a few months to my initial infection by the punk germ. It is only by observing the baby bacteria squirming on the petri dish that we can understand how it all took hold and how its tendrils slithered through the rest of my (still in progress at press time) life.

I came into rock and its offshoots around age fifteen. My parents had a tenuous acceptance of the more conservative types of music and disdain for the rest of it. I grew up with a transistor radio and a tape recorder. Over the years some songs pushed a pop button in my head and led me to like tracks by The Beatles, Ramones, Clash, Cheap Trick, and a smattering of '70s and '80s pop hits, once considered disposable and now quotation mark bracketed "classics." I drew no connections between these bands. To me, they were just groups who made sounds that appealed to a brain lacking any real reference points or pre-conceptions.

It was Pink Floyd's *The Wall* that exposed me to angsty rock. Immediately, a heavy oak door opened in my yearning teenage think-sponge and allowed in the rainbow light of '60s and '70s psychedelia and progressive (prog, kids, prog) rock. This was not the manufactured pop perfection (horns, treble, no low-end) of the mid-80s, but the iconoclastic defiance of bygone days I merely caught a whiff of as the Age of Aquarius curdled on the periphery of my pre-adolescent perception.

Psych and prog gave me a new stance. It wasn't just horror movies and books for me. Now I was part of some secret handshake club (membership: one eager twig of a boy). My posse consisted of Syd Barrett, Jon Anderson, Robert Fripp, and a bat-winged Peter Gabriel, so how could any Bon Jovi meatheads possibly compare to my mellotron-drenched coolness?

And then there was James. James had been my pen pal for years, thanks to a classified ad in a monster magazine. Our means of communication were audio cassettes. We'd blab and blab to each other, then mail the tapes off, eagerly awaiting the next volley. James was several years older than me and capable of belting out multi-tape aural epics. He had lived in Hawaii, but was now serving in the Air Force and claiming to see Lovecraftian monsters above his bed when he went to sleep. (James would later profess his heavily closeted homosexuality and illicit psychedelic drug use.) When I went through my transformation from horror-obsessive to decidedly drugless acid-rock enthusiast, he took a certain glee in watching my fragile wings unfold.

Along for the ride was my brother Bull, three years my junior, who also religiously listened to the James tapes and attempted to contribute a word here and there. Bull was leaving his *Miami Vice* phase and was fully immersed in BMX biking. He could pop a mean endo with his sizable group of friends. Meanwhile, I was a glistening fungus with the requisite aversions to sunlight and the accusatory fingers of fresh air.

What began as a minor threat from James ("In the next set of tapes I'm going to tape you some *real* music…the Sex Pistols!"), became the most anticipated event of the year. I had heard of this Sex Pistols band, but in my mind it was all…well…filth and fury. Surely nothing that came from a bunch of safety-pinned losers could ever speak to me like a side-long song with a lute solo, right?

When the tapes arrived, they were an arrow into my brain. He teased us with a couple jokey tracks from the *Great Rock 'n' Roll Swindle* soundtrack then hit us hard with a few songs from *Never Mind the Bollocks*. I was knocked firmly on my ass and left furtively grasping for the nearest safety pin. There was all of my teenage anger distilled and fermented into pop-length songs, with a sneer that still seethed ten years on. While the Pistols and their ilk were never to supersede my precious psychedelic troubadours, they proceeded to keep close quarters with them from then on.

Post Pistol-bomb—a bomb whose force exploded with such an impact that it fragmentized my brother as well—we went on to seek out every band with any fetid hint of the punk. From the essential (Black Flag, MDC, Youth Brigade) to the decidedly dodgy (The Exploited and, uhhh... Grong Grong), we procured whatever our meager allowances would allow us to purchase, often choosing one band's record because we saw a picture of a member of another band wearing their t-shirt. (Those huge record sleeve insert collages from Combat and Metal Blade Records of bands wearing a different thrash band's shirt in each tiny picture was like catalog shopping for us. Bands like Nuclear Assault, Ludichrist, and Cryptic Slaughter sure owned a lot of cool shirts!) The direct leftist politics of the most incendiary of the bands led us to believe that punk was a still-vital insurrectionist movement composed of kids just like us. President Ronald Reagan must have been shaking in his shoes every time DRI played "Reaganomics."

When my stoner friends wrangled up a car to drive to North Philly to see my straight edge, near-hippie heroes, 7 Seconds, I almost peed in my jean shorts. Now I could be the New Wind, whoah, whoah. Getting my parents (who were none-too-enthused with my new found love of f-word laden noise) to agree to allow me to go with a group of longhairs (one of whom was even black) out of the working class suburbs of NJ to head for big, bad Philthadelphia was no small task. But I was a good kid with decent grades and no secret drinking or drug use, so there was no reason not to trust me. To their credit, they did.

Suited up in the punkest attire I could manage, I popped into the bathroom to—I dunno—practice a quick sneer or something, while my father was in the shower. From the shower stall Dad bellowed, "You're not going to be *slam*-dancing, are you?" His distinctly hyphenated use of a compound word I didn't think he was cognizant of struck me—shaking in anticipation and fear for the forthcoming rejection the night could bring—as the funniest goddamn thing I had ever heard.

***

Hours later I was finally there, in the arena of hardcore where the kids would be united in order to never be divided. The first disappointment came when I found out that 7 Seconds was a no-show. Then there were the kids themselves. They weren't exactly there to raise their consciousness: they were there, as my father said, to *slam*-dance. I stood at the edge of the pit and watched the punkest minds of my generation beat the fucking shit out of each other. I thought I had made a great mistake. Surely, this was not the world for me?

With no 7 Seconds, I still saw Justice League, the Philly legends Scram and, presumably, Fail-Safe. The details nearly twenty years on are all rather vague. At other shows at Club Pizazz, I would witness skinheads macing dancers, punks versus skins parking lot bottle fights, and all that came with the turbulent pre-Nirvana punk scene. I eventually found the elements in punk concerned with social and political change. The timeline, from nervously stepping in the door of a crap disco club that was renting to the punks for a Friday night show, to hosting my own shows (along with my brother and others) that more closely mirrored my ethics, was a short one. Punk was like that for us: we couldn't stand on the sidelines for long before we had to be active members.

James successfully sowed the seed of dissent in me, but as I moved from a nervy sixteen-year-old to a more confident adult, I drifted away from him. He navigated his way out of the Air Force and embraced his homosexuality, eventually taking on the job of a giant, life-sized animal at Disney World. I don't think he ever fully understood the impact of the Sex Pistols songs he teasingly placed on a C-90 for two South Jersey boys.

Hardcore punk was an infection that proved incurable. For years I wore its fevered blisters like a badge of honor. In time, the infection would recede a trifle, the fever dissipating, yet never allowing my temperature to return to an acceptable 98.6 degrees. Every thought, every decision, every moral or ethical judgment must first pass through the prism of punk particles still lodged in my head and heart. What comes out isn't always a spectrum of beautiful light, but at least it's not the sad shades of grey of those who've never been clocked on the head with a combat boot while trying to finger point and chant their way through a youth anthem. Those who have been there realize one thing: yesterday's youth anthem is today's requiem. *Enjoy it while it fucking lasts.*

LOVE IS A BATTLEFIELD

Darren Walters

While, in truth, the event that I am about to write about was not my first show (which featured local Philadelphia legends the Dead Milkmen), but my second, it is not only a better story, but it is also more akin to the shows that I would attend from this point onwards in the mid-80s and had a greater bearing on my future in punk rock than any other.

It was early October of 1986. In the state of Delaware, the driving age was sixteen and, while I was of age as of August that year, I had yet to attain my driver's license for a variety of reasons. Having been intro-duced into punk rock more than two years prior, my friends and I had not been able to attend shows in the relatively close city of Philadelphia, due to the lack of licenses in our group. Not only did this put a serious damper on our punk rock credibility, but it compounded our thirst to see a real punk band in the flesh. Sure, we had seen The Cure and other such acts at big arenas, and interacted with others of our kind, but what we were craving was the kind of show that we saw in *Decline of the Western Civilization* or *Suburbia*.

At this time, my hair was a strange mix of the Tony Hawk skate cut and an unattended mess: it was shaved on the right side and the rest of the hair swooped down over my left eye and was long in the back. I had just bleached it out and my parents were not too happy. My outfit was a prerequisite black overcoat, a black button-up shirt, black jeans, a bunch of odd jewelry, and topped off with my blue high-top Chuck Taylor All-Stars kicks (with DK, MDC, DI, etc. all etched into the material).

I was a junior in high school and dating a brunette named Suzy, the then love of my life, who for all of her pseudo-preppy exterior, reminded me of a younger Siouxsie Sioux. She had a grim sense of humor, a defiant wit, and made damn sure that she always got her way. I dare say that I loved her from the moment we met while riding the bus and discussing the merits of the Sex Pistols' UK influence versus the East Bay antics of the Dead Kennedys.

Suzy was the kind of girlfriend that you wanted, hesitantly, when you are sixteen. She was always daring me, testing to see if I could withstand the heat. Suzy would drink more than me, dare me to fight for her honor, and was driven to make a young man crazy by exploiting his willingness to go to any lengths to prove his desires.

So, of course it was Suzy who would suggest that our mutual friend Cindy and I make the leap to go to City Gardens in Trenton, NJ to see Last Stand, Agnostic Front, and the Circle Jerks. Cindy made perfect sense in the equation: being a year older than both Suzy and I, she had a car and a license, and would be more than willing to go for the thrill of it all. After the plan was agreed to, I recall having the gut-wrenching feeling that I would remember the show for as long as I lived.

Trenton was only an hour and some change away from our homes, but we left with plenty of time to spare so that we could soak up as much of the atmosphere as possible. It was not Suzy or Cindy's first shows either. Cindy was a bit more experienced than both Suzy and I in terms of going to shows, but Suzy had already seen Suicidal Tendencies when she lived in Alabama, so I figured that she would be rather nonplussed by anything that we might encounter in New Jersey.

When we arrived at the venue, a first time for all of us, I was scared shitless. The parking lot was packed with skinheads, punks, and freaks of all types. Beer drinkers and dope smokers, party animals and peace punks. Whatever existed at the time, there was at least one caricature in attendance to pay homage to the scene or belief system. In hindsight, it was a critical moment in the '80s, prior to the strict segregation of punks into one sub-genre or another.

Everyone at the gig looked bigger, older, and meaner than me—and that immediately put me ill at ease. I was a suburban boy through and through, and City Gardens was located in one of the toughest areas of Trenton. I was a nervous wreck. I knew that this was going to be a long night, and I attempted to steady myself in order to vanquish the pit that was developing in the bottom of my stomach. Here I was, without any of my dudes, at a show that I knew would make me a true punk, if only I could get through it unscathed and back home safely.

Sticking together, we entered and waded into the large City Gardens room. It was a wide-open space with a large stage and a bar set farther back in the room: the perfect venue. At the time, City Gardens still kept some small tables and chairs on the main floor. These were already taken, so I searched for a safe haven elsewhere.

The show was packed. My eyes eagerly darted around the room to find a safe haven for my girlfriend, and well...more importantly, myself.

I was quick to spot a set of bleachers to our left and decided they would be a good, safe location. As Last Stand began their Revolution Summer/7 Seconds style rock, I escorted the women up to the top row. At first we all stood, soaking everything up. I began to relax as I grooved to Last Stand, who were my type of punk—I even liked them enough to buy their record. Little did I know at the time that they would be the most tame band on the bill.

Pleased that the show had thus far been enjoyable and without event, I was finally beginning to relax. In no way was I prepared for what came next, as the almighty Agnostic Front emerged to take the stage. These tough motherfuckers and their rabid followers (many who had traveled from nearby NYC) terrified me right from the start. Not only did they look scary and intimidating, but they also had loads of tattoos and plenty of attitude. While I was aware of who Agnostic Front were, the NYC scene hadn't really broke out and made an impact in Delaware yet, where we were more into following the DC-style of punk, like Faith and Marginal Man.

As soon as singer, Roger Miret, grabbed the mic, the skinhead volcano erupted and a steady flow of skin brothers and sisters rushed up front, covering the landscape with shiny, bald heads.

Agnostic Front's *Cause For Alarm* album had just come out, and Agnostic Front had become more metallic and speed driven. To top it off, Cliff Burton from Metallica had just died the week or so before, so Agnostic Front dedicated their entire set to him. I may be wrong, but I remember them doing a few Metallica covers during their set that night. What I do know for certain is that AF were very metal that night, more so than in any of the dozens of times that I would see them since, and the crowd responded by fucking shit up. The skins went nutso. All set long they took the dance floor as their battlefield and dared the unshaven to enter the pit.

As I quivered from my perch above, I saw a skinhead fall backwards, hitting his head on a table as he fell to the floor. Blood splashed everywhere as his skull exploded upon impact with the hardwood floor. Next, a random punk, who was fairly large, took the pit bait and punched a skin in the face, breaking his nose instantly. I wish that I could say that was the worst of it. The violence was plentiful, seemingly endless, and strangely carefree. As the body count rose with each song, I tried to hold hands with Suzy without seeming anxious about the odds of us leaving alive. Suzy loved it! And there I was, terrified and pissing my pants. Somehow I knew this was going to be the most violent and bloody show that I would ever see.

When the blazing Agnostic Front finally completed their set, I advocated that maybe we shouldn't stay for the rest of the show. I had seen enough and I wanted to get back to my safe suburban enclave before my virgin eyes took in any more violence. And while I loved the Circle Jerks, their set just wasn't something that I thought was wise to stick around for. The girls laughed and thought I was trying to be funny. I grasped the opportunity and chuckled, brushing it off as a mere gas.

Finally, after two hours of waiting, the Circle Jerks came on and the circle pit started. As all of the Mohicans and skaters hauled ass for the developing pit, Suzy and Cindy leapt down off of the bleachers and landed smack in the middle of hurricane Skank. I ran after them in a panic; I thought they would get eaten alive in this crowd.

As they entered the pit, I lost sight of them both and tentatively stood at the edge trying to identify them in the swirl of boneheads and liberty spikes. All of a sudden, someone grabbed my hand and into the pit I went. Luckily, it was Suzy who was whirling me about. We flew around in a whirlwind of sweaty skin and smoky clothes. Being a stupid kid, I finally let go and went with the flow of traffic. My introduction to the social ritual of the pit only lasted until the end of the song. Huffing at the outskirts of the circle, Suzy and I smiled at each other, giggling at our shared experience. Not only had we both "pitted it up," but we did so together, and thus, our night was complete.

Suzy and I eventually moved back to our spot on the bleachers. Having reconnected with Cindy, we all watched the Circle Jerks from our perfect vantage point.

The Circle Jerks continued to play and more fights broke out as City Gardens' floor soaked up the blood. The show never ceased to be violent, it only ebbed and flowed—so much so, that we all finally agreed it might be a good idea to leave before the Circle Jerks were finished.

As the three of us walked back to Cindy's car, I could hear the Circle Jerks banging out hit after hit. I didn't care at this point, as the girls and I were just happy to be alive. We had experienced one hell of a show—that much we all agreed upon. I was ecstatic that Suzy and I had slammed together, and that I could tell everyone about going out of state to see a show. As I climbed into Cindy's car, I smiled about the three of us, smashed up in to the front seat of the big Buick: together as friends, lovers, and punks.

Looking back, I had an amazing time. It's one of the few shows that I will never forget and in fact, as evidenced above, remember vividly. I'm not sure how it shaped me into becoming the person I am today, but I do know that after that City Gardens show, it took me another two years before I would go to see Agnostic Front again. By that time, seeing AF at City Gardens was an even more dangerous endeavor because of the serious Nazi skinhead problem that took over New Jersey in the late-80s. Another interesting note is that I went to see the Circle Jerks three or four other times in the '80s and at each and every show, something happened which prevented me from ever seeing a complete Circle Jerks show to this day.

PUNK SLASH GOTH

Michelle Tea

The *Boston Phoenix* was the coolest paper and if you went to certain locations in Boston, like the Berklee College of Music, where there was a box office that sold concert tickets, and outside boys with long, mis-shapen hairdos smoked cigarettes in the cold, you could grab a paper for free. I liked having this in, since the thing cost a dollar fifty, but it also gave me just the slightest twinge of anxiety—like, how come a kid who can afford to go to a sort of expensive music college gets the *Phoenix* for free? I felt doomed to the class that never got anything for free and always had to work harder than anyone. That was my family. Everyone was a nurse, the kind that took care of dying old people. People with Alzheimer's, who lost their brains and shit themselves. My family worked at VA hospitals and corporate-owned nursing homes. They took care of these *vegetables* all day, got harassed and unappreciated by the manage-ment and came home at night, exhausted, to chain smoke and eat boxed food while watching *Family Ties* and *Growing Pains*. Complaints, in between commercials, always boiled down to a couple of sentiments: People with money were horrible, and should they—my parents—slide into the sort of physical and mental disrepair their charges suffered, Do Not Resusci-tate. *A bottle of Seconal and a six-pack.* No big funeral, either. *Just toss me into a Hefty bag.* None of that fancy coffin shit. No wonder I became a sort of angry goth and my sister an overachieving student slash cheer-leader slash beauty pageant queen. It'd have to have been one or the other.

Inside the *Boston Phoenix* were lots of things. Articles about things that were cool that I hadn't known about. Political stuff and music. Per-sonal ads. Escort ads. I would get all tangled up on the inside just reading the little squares of innuendo. I'd call the numbers. A woman would an-swer, and I'd slam the phone down. My baby blue plastic telephone with the frayed wire that often ruined my phone calls. I'd crank call hookers,

then hop into bed and masturbate furiously. What a creep. I was about
fifteen, sixteen years old. I had big, teased hair. I liked punk, or goth, or
whatever the fuck I liked, because you couldn't ruin it. It was already
ruined. That was the point. You started at the bottom, looking like shit.
Your hair was a mess. You couldn't put your lipstick on straight. Who
fucking cared? You cared? Fuck you. Punk was getting to say fuck you
all the time, getting to say fuck you first, throwing the first punch. Even
though I was such a wimp. People flung things at me for looking like such
a wreck. My backcombed hair—weird, spotty bleach-y colors, then black,
then the arduous bleach back from black, that trip through burnt orange,
nicotine yellow, then it would be ready for the pinks and the purples and
reds. Out of car windows came projectiles aimed at my giant poof of
hairdo. Empty bottles, an empty milk carton. A nice old fashioned rock.
My lips were black, or a pearlescent blue, like the lips of dead people.
My mother, who took care of the half-dead all day, did not understand
why her daughter was trying to look like one of them. She hollered and
screamed. My hair was trashed, it resembled a mushroom cloud. My
skin was coated in white grease paint and baby powder. The more goth
I got, the less punk, the more precision seemed to be required with the
makeup. Those elegant lines of black around the eyes. I had to keep a
foot in punk so I could get away with my smears and smudges. I didn't
have the knack for elegance, didn't have the patience to care. Perfection was oppressive. Beauty, too. Money was oppressive. My mother was
wicked oppressive. We fought in the haze of her cigarette smoke and
hopefully I wouldn't end up grounded and confined to my room. Trapped
in Chelsea, unable to get into Boston where the other punk slash goth
kids were. If I was really punk I would've screamed *fuck you* and broke
a dish against the wall and stormed out in my boots. Instead I sobbed
in my room, Depeche Mode on the stereo. Unless the stereo had been
taken away as punishment—the worst punishment. I would lay and weep
to *Black Celebration*. I guess I was goth after all. An art fag. I tried to cut
my arm, but it didn't really do anything for me. I felt like a phony. I pulled
a section of the *Boston Phoenix* out from under my bed and poured
through the listings. Where would I go when my punishment ended. I
anticipated its end to arrive, approximately, tomorrow. My mother had a
terrible rage, a huge fear of my appearance and behavior, but no staying
power when it came to discipline. I knew that no matter what happened,
the next day I would put back on whatever outfit had offended her and

leave the house. I guess that meant I won. I always won, which didn't mean that life didn't suck.

Most of the all-ages shows I'd been to were, I don't know, no one used the word *alternative* yet, but that's what they were. Indie-pop. Ball and Pivot were a band I really liked but they weren't punk. The boys all looked like girls, or fags. I loved that. The lead singer's orange hair and inflated lips. His orange hair tumbled down his pale pale face luxuriously. His name was B, just the letter, and I loved him when I was fifteen. Ball and Pivot shows were a lot of hormonal girls just learning how to style themselves. Everyone was sort of gasping and awkward and posing. Lots of cigarette smoking. There was another show happening, at the Channel. On Sunday afternoons at the Channel there were often all-ages punk shows. The Channel wasn't in brainy, artsy Cambridge like the Ball and Pivot show. The Channel was some old warehousy building squat on the edge of the water. The harbor bashed up against its backside, and the air smelled like dirty brine. There was a wide parking lot and, beyond that, a bunch of indecipherable buildings. Businesses closed for the weekend, maybe; offices or warehouses, shipping and receiving, maybe people lived in some of them, I don't know, that part of town seemed shut down. No place to eat or get something to drink, no place to shop. I didn't have the money to shop anywhere but Goodwill mostly, and records of course, but still I liked to be around where things were sold, the bustle of other people spending their money. It made me feel like I was in the world, the stream of life, though I guess it was just commerce. I liked it, even if I was making fun of it. Being obnoxious in the face of Newbury Street shoppers, drunk and hollering, but I always marked my progress down the street by the clothing in the windows, the giant dresses hung on sulking mannequins. Pausing before a lit window and gazing at the insides, my boozy breath fogging the glass. The same way I'd gaze at a big-haired boy on the subway. I was in love with this dress, a fluffy one with a big skirt and lace. It probably cost a million dollars. I loved Newbury Street and all the things I could never have. I loved the million dollar dresses and hated only the women who could have them, who never would deserve them like I did. Not so punk, wanting the dresses. I'm pretty sure I was goth, really.

The show at the Channel was full of boys. And none of them were wearing makeup. I thought the whole point of punk was to have a boyfriend who wore as much makeup as I did. We could kiss and it wouldn't be a big deal because our makeup would already be smeared. We could drink too much and cry together and it wouldn't be a big deal because our eyemakeup was already halfway down out cheeks. The band that played at this show was called Gang Green. I tried to like it. I didn't want to be such a wimp all the time, so unpunk. I tried to find the melody, couldn't catch it. Duh, it was punk, there's no melody. Maybe I wasn't punk after all. The thought was so disappointing. I wanted to be punk so bad. Ever since I was twelve, thirteen, I'd been waiting to get a little bit older and have this punk life. But this music sucked. A loud roar, braying, like a pile of frat boys too drunk and screaming together at a sports game. The boys at the show looked like they could be at the sports game, some of them. Others looked okay. They had mohawks and stuff, that was cool. Not so many girls, and the ones that were there looked at me and my girl-friends like maybe they'd like to murder us. I guess we didn't look so punk, in our neo-victorian thriftwear. I consoled myself with the Sex Pistols. I *loved* the Sex Pistols. They were the punkest ever. They invented punk. If I liked them—loved them—then I was punk, too. Siouxsie Sioux was around for all that, too. She was part of it. And she was the ultimate goth. See, goth was punk. Siouxsie was the bridge, punk to goth, and she was a girl, so fuck off. This show sucked. They were singing about beer. I liked to get drunk too, but singing about beer seemed stupid. But then, I always preferred vodka. We left before someone kicked our asses.

NIGHT AT THE LONGMARCH

George Hurchalla

My introduction to live punk rock came during the fall of 1983. Having just turned seventeen years old, I was in my first year of college, outside Philadelphia. There had been no punk scene in my small hometown in Florida, so while I had been listening to punk and hardcore for the past three years, I had not had the chance to see bands play. I took the train into Philadelphia from my college in the suburbs, alighted in Center City, and took the Broad Street line down to South Street. A six-band extravaganza was taking place on the second floor of an old building called Longmarch Hall, on the corner of Broad and South, opposite where the short-lived punk venue, Love Hall, had stood. A jazz club called Longmarch Jazz Academy had opened for one night at the location, but someone got stabbed and the venue was never used again until punks discovered it and started putting on shows there. I went to the show completely naïve, looking forward to slam dancing for the first time. The line-up was Rude Awakening (Delaware), Y-DI (Philly), Iron Cross (DC), Void (DC), Antidote (New York), and Necros (Ohio).

There were punks coming in from hundreds of miles away—State College, Harrisburg, North Jersey, New York, DC—for one of the first big hardcore gatherings in Philly since the legendary Buff Hall show over in Camden where Minor Threat and SS Decontrol had played. Eric DeJesus, who published the zine *Raw Pogo on the Scaffold*, remembers it being the first time he came to Philadelphia, rolling in with a crew of punks from the Lehigh Valley. The Lehigh Valley punks got there five hours too early, but Jim McMonagle of Flag of Democracy recognized one of them as his double-decker, chicken-fight slamming partner from a Dead Kennedys show, and sent them in the direction of the local record stores. "We met NY dudes who hitched freight trains down to that show," DeJesus told me. "That kinda stuff sealed it for me. From then on, I was full-on hardcore for the next couple of years."

While none of the bands stood out as "names" to me at the time, the show went down in history in Philly as one of the landmark punk rock events. Each of the bands had fanatic followings. There was an elaborate etiquette to slam dancing that had to be followed to make the seemingly violent chaos of it harmless to the participants. It couldn't work with only a half dozen people in a large pit—which was sometimes the case during this show. My first slam dancing attempts make me cringe in retrospect. I was ignorant of these nuances. My understanding was that it was like a game of human bumper cars or demolition derby, in which you chose a target on the other side of the floor from you, charged full tilt into him and then did it again to someone else. I remember doing this and knocking a mystified kid half my size on his ass, grinning broadly at him, helping him to his feet, and charging off again. I was an idiot, but a friendly one. Luckily the scene at Longmarch was not very cohesive, and I was very tall, or I would have deservedly gotten my ass kicked.

The bands inspired nothing less than complete abandon. Y-DI was one of the most powerful Philly hardcore bands, fronted by their imposing black singer, Jackal. The band had made a strong impression on Bob Mould when Hüsker Dü came through, and he mentioned them and Void as two of his favorite East Coast bands around that time.

"Our show always had an aura of intense violence that we projected on stage," recalled Jackal on the *Hardcore Hall of Fame* website. "The violent energy that came from us was not maliciously directed at anyone in particular. It was a release of all the pent up shit of being poor, isolated, misunderstood, and hated by the general population. So when we went on stage we would just let all this shit go! The audience would feel our hate and go fucking berserk. Arms flailing, boots stomping, and bodies crashing!"

Void was legendary for the power of their live shows. Like Scream, they were one of the early Dischord bands that only found themselves halfway accepted in the DC scene because of being from the suburbs—in their case, Columbia, Maryland. While Dischord put them out on a split LP with The Faith, they found that when it came to being put on the bills for shows in the city, they were sometimes treated as outsiders. Out of DC, though, they were making a much bigger impression initially than a lot of the other bands. Throughout the nation they had rabid fans. They were one of the first bands to have a thrash metal sound, and the blistering fervor of Bubba Dupree's guitar work left a lot of punks in awe. The memories of Eric DeJesus, captured at the time in *Raw Pogo on the Scaffold*, are much more vivid than my distant memories and I leave it to him to capture the atmosphere:

"It is all so fucking beautiful and crowded in the gigantic Longmarch," wrote DeJesus in *Raw Pogo*. "It is terrifying and real. I cannot breathe. The only place you can see anything is from the sides of the stage with seventy other little kids pushing and shoving and acting psychotic because VOID IS ABOUT TO START! And Void are the only band that can scare me. And Void are the only band that get the children of the East Coast to ape the criminally insane."

My concession to wearing something of a punk uniform, which started at this show, was to scrawl the names of each of my favorite bands that I'd gotten to see on a white t-shirt with red magic marker. The shirt was quickly torn up while slamming, thus instantly becoming all the more punk. Each scene brought a different style, which DeJesus described in *Raw Pogo*:

> I got the old man MacGregor golf jacket with the plaid inside and the LVHC symbol safety-pinned on the back. I got the old style Carolina combat boots spray-painted black. I got the rolled up Beaver Cleaver jeans and the Sugsy crew cut happening. I traced the entire *Still Screaming* LP cover on my white tee with the lyrics too. The North Jersey people look like garbage men. The DC people show up and everyone turns and looks. They style in clean leather jackets, they got the XXX on the back, and long, long sleeping caps with the pom-pom on the end.

Iron Cross had a strong following devoted to their slower Oi sound, but in my early throes of thrash passion I found them a little sedate compared to the fury of the other bands. Necros had an energetic little bowling ball of a singer, Barry Henssler, who was a dynamo. He looked like a funny little fat Midwestern kid who had stuck his finger in an electrical socket and gone berserk. Corey Rusk, the bassist, was responsible for the zine *Smegma Journal* and had started the legendary indie label Touch and Go before he was even eighteen years old. With better equipment than the other bands and more experience, the power of Necros was formidable. The crowd truly went insane during their set.

I took the train out to the suburbs late that night, a sweaty and wide-eyed mess. Punk in the big city and I had met, and it was the beginning of some of the best years of my life.

NAILED TO THE X

Kyle Metzner

"Three kids died on this bridge last month," Devon said. "They were headed to a show at the Anthrax." This is how Devon began his gruesome tale of a car full of punks losing control of their automobile on the slick metal bridge we were driving over. As the bridge sang its hollow whistle song, he pointed out the jerky dance that the metal grating produced in our car. Like the doomed punks, we were also headed to the Anthrax, a club in Connecticut so legendary to me that it was hardly surprising to find a protective death bridge standing guard.

It was 1989, and as a freshman in high school, I was still a year away from a driver's license. The wandering effect that metal grating has on a car is something I'd have to take Devon's word for. He was five years older than me and treated me like a younger brother. I met him after answering an ad he placed in the back of *Maximum RocknRoll* about starting a chapter of Positive Force, modeled after the activist group of the same name out of Washington, DC. Devon lived in the same town as my dad, whom I visited every other weekend, so I got a ride over to his apartment one day for the first meeting of Positive Force CT.

I quietly knocked on Devon's apartment door and when he answered, sporting a 7 Seconds tattoo on his arm, I was hugely impressed. He said flatly, "So are you in high school or something?" We hung out at his desk for a while and talked about music, and when it was clear that no one else was showing up for the meeting, we started. Devon grabbed a spiral bound notebook and sat across from me in a chair. I didn't have a notebook or a pen, or even a vague idea of what we would do as a Positive Force chapter.

"So what kinds of local issues do you want to tackle in your town?" Devon asked. I was a bit stunned by this question. I quickly realized that we weren't just going to sit around and listen to DC punk all afternoon. My mind raced for an answer. Local issues? Would "we must be united, fight the good fight" be an appropriate response? Apartheid in South Africa was about as local as my issues got. Show me a hundred hardcore kids from 1989 and I'll show you at least four bloody, explosion-filled fantasies about springing Nelson Mandela from prison.

"There's racism." I said.

"Ok." He said. "Anything specific?"

"Uh…Hmm… There's also corruption." I said. Devon tapped the pen on his knee. He was realizing that I was a "big picture" kind of guy.

"Hey, you wanna help me collate my zine?" he asked.

"Fuck yeah!"

So we stapled, listened to music, drank coffee, and made plans to hang out the next time I visited my dad. When Devon called a few days later to invite me to see Supertouch with him at the Anthrax, I was so excited that I could barely say "yes." My friends and I had been staring at photos from the Anthrax for years. Every fanzine out of the Northeast featured at least a couple of photos from the place. I would be the first explorer from my crew to step foot on this hallowed ground. My first show was going to be like the moon landing—a dangerous and exciting fact-finding mission.

Devon picked me up a week later in his old Tercel, and we sped off toward the Anthrax. His car was the first non-parent car I ever rode in. I felt really comfortable in it. It reminded me of my bedroom: there were band stickers everywhere, piles of well-read zines in the back seat, empty

Jolt cans rolling around on the floor, and stacks of cassette tapes on the dashboard.

After traversing the metal death bridge and driving for another half hour, we finally pulled into the parking lot of the club. I couldn't believe how many kids were hanging out, waiting for the doors to open. I had never seen so many people wearing hoodies in the same place before. They were like an army. Instead of noticing the disturbing level of conformity, I saw a crowd of druids getting ready to don their hoods and do something magical.

The Anthrax parking lot was dimly lit, but I could clearly make out the poses and body language that I recognized from record covers and videos. There were lots of arms crossed in strong conviction. There were feet planted firmly on the ground. (Not too far apart, yet not too close together.) There were kids sitting hunched on the steps with their hoods pulled low over their faces, creating shadows that camouflaged their looks of righteous determination. Surveying this scene was like watching a familiar painting or photograph come suddenly to life. These were the poses that seeped out of your record crate and into your head while you slept in your suburban basement.

Devon turned off the car and pulled a Sharpie marker out of the glove box. He drew a thick, black "X" on the back of each of his hands, signifying his commitment to the drug-free, straight edge lifestyle. I'd been devouring straight edge zines and records for years, so I knew all about the Xs on the hands, but the thing about zines is that they can be six months to a year old by the time they make it into your eager hands. The photos in them might be even older than that. I was definitely straight edge and felt passionate and idealistic about it, but I wasn't totally sure whether kids were still wearing Xs or not. I surveyed the parking lot, looking for Xs. Fuck, it was too dark to see. Devon passed the marker to me low, keeping it out of sight of the crowd, like he was passing a joint or something. Maybe he wanted them to think his hands were always marked up. I held the Sharpie and craned my neck around, looking for an X. I just wanted to see one other X. It wasn't that I thought Devon was uncool, or that he didn't know what was up. I just couldn't bear the thought of being ostracized from this garden of eden before I even got across the parking lot. It's one thing to walk with a friend into a room full of people when you both have your pants cuffed in last year's style, it's a whole different thing when you and this friend are the only ones with huge black Xs scrawled on your hands. I stalled a bit longer, until a van pulled up and blocked my view of the crowd. I took a deep breath, uncapped the Sharpie, and committed to the X. True till death.

Devon and I walked up to the door as everyone started filing in. I kept my hands in my pockets. My plan was to keep my hands there for the entire show if it turned out that we were the only dorks with Xs. Luckily, once we got inside, I saw that most kids had Xs on their hands. They were all drawn in different styles. It was like viewing the results from one of those psychology tests where you draw a self-portrait and then have your personality interpreted by the thickness of your pen lines.

Inside the Anthrax, I walked close to the walls, checking out the layers of graffiti scrawl and stickers everywhere. As I watched everyone around me giddily assemble into little groups, I started feeling awkward without my friends. I liked Devon, but I barely knew him, and he was five years older than me. I wished I had my own group there. I wanted to laugh and be as obnoxious as everyone else, but when you do it alone, you just look sort of crazy. I had the feeling of being the outsider at the beach who tries to get close to the locals over a week-long summer trip. You end up hanging out near them, but it's obvious to anyone watching that you're not actually accepted by them.

When the first band started tuning up, everyone crammed in tight, and any conflicted thoughts of belonging or acceptance fell away. We quickly turned into one huge mass of blurred boundaries. I looked around at all the excited faces pushing tighter and tighter together, and thought, "Where the hell are all the girls?" There were probably three in the whole place. It's true that the photos I'd seen in zines always showed crowds of guys with their fists in the air, but I always thought it was because of the camera angle. Maybe if the photographer backed up just a hair, we'd see groups of girls with their fists up outside of the pit. Unfortunately, the camera didn't lie. This definitely sucked, because I concluded before coming, that if I couldn't find a potential girlfriend at a hardcore show, amongst my own people, then I'd never find one.

When the band finally lunged into their set, the crowd turned into an ocean. The chaos and tumult of a hundred lives spilled together into this living thing that pushed and pulled and sometimes struck back with fury. The undertow dragged me down with the chug-chug bass and a tentacled beast lifted me back up. The ocean tossed me around. It made me laugh my ass off. It compelled me to grab the arms of strangers while I fell. I didn't ask permission or apologize.

Over time I'd make friends with the people in this room, and the ocean would grow to be something even larger and more uncontrollable. Into this is where we would throw our beliefs, no matter how half-baked or ill-formed, and watch them collide and mutate and sometimes break. The best thing about the ocean was that it was ours. We had a motherfucking ocean.

LAND OF HOPE AND GLORY

Bull Gervasi

Sometime in 1986, my brother Joseph and I received a monumental cassette tape from our then-penpal, James. A few years earlier Joseph and he found each other through a classified ad in the back of a horror film magazine. James lived in Hawaii and was in his mid-thirties. Joseph and I lived in the south Jersey suburbs of Philadelphia and were fifteen and twelve, respectively. At some point we started exchanging tapes instead of writing. These tapes would often include songs along with our ramblings. Little did we know that James' decision to include "Anarchy in the UK" by the Sex Pistols would change the course of our young lives.

As soon as we heard it we were hooked! Luckily the record store in our neighborhood had the Sex Pistols *Nevermind the Bollocks…* LP in stock. Otherwise, we would have come to a quick dead end as there were no other record stores in our area and the Internet didn't arrive at our parent's house for another fifteen years. Going to the record store quickly became an obsession of ours. Up until then, most of our exposure to music came via our uncle. Uncle Mike lived in the "Greg Brady" attic room at our grandparent's house. His room was covered in posters and he had a giant sparkly gold double bass Slingerland drum set. He played us his favorite prog and classic rock records. This is where we developed a taste for heavy music.

At the record store, we would buy any record with a "punk" looking cover. We'd analyze the "thank you" lists and photos for clues about other cool bands to look out for. Along the way, we discovered some really great bands and some not so good ones. Also, we found *Maximum RocknRoll* magazine, which enlightened us to the fact that there was a huge punk scene out there, somewhere. My brother got to know a few punks at his high school who told him about shows in Philly. I wasn't allowed to go to shows for about another six months. Otherwise, my first punk show would have been 7 Seconds (see Joseph's story elsewhere in this book).

It was December, 1987. My mom drove us to the train that ran between south Jersey and Philly. This was my only ticket out of New Jersey until I had friends that drove. On this train ride, we met a whole cast of characters from the NJ punk scene. One of them was this guy Brian, who some months later, took us record shopping in the basement of the Third Street Jazz and Rock in Philly, there he suggested his favorite bands to us. Later that day, we had our first run in with Nazi skinheads and had to hide out in Zipperhead (memorialized in the song "Punk Rock Girl" by The Dead Milkmen).

Once we got to Philly, we switched trains to head to the Northeast, getting off at the Margaret/Orthodox stop in Frankford. We had no idea where we were going, blindly following all the other punks into some uncharted territory far from home. It wasn't until the mid-90s that I figured out where the hell this place really was.

Club Pizzazz was a little, two story dance club with a shitty paint job in an old working class neighborhood. I was dressed in the punk-est outfit that I could come up with: a pair of gray Bugle Boy pants, an army jacket that I drew the cover of *Walk Together, Rock Together* on the back of, and a pair of Chucks. The club was small and packed with people bigger, and seemingly, way older than me. All the studs, spikes, mohawks, boots, and angst-y dudes were intimidating. But even though I was scared, it was exhilarating to witness something so different from anything else I'd experienced at that point. And then the bands played! The lineup of the show was classic: Misunderstood (NJ), F.O.D. (Philly—they still play!), Government Issue (DC), and Verbal Assault (RI). I remember being excited by F.O.D.'s sense of humor while they played. They made some joke about moshed potatoes and threw potatoes into the crowd. It was a relief to see all the punks laughing. This environment made sense, as I never felt like I fit in with other kids my age, especially since I wasn't into sports. I knew this would become my "scene." G.I. played next, and I remember liking them, but not much more at that point. Because it was a school night and mom and dad didn't want us out too late, I only got to see a few songs by Verbal Assault (who later became a great influence on my band, Policy of 3). It was great to see bands perform live and feel the energy of the show. Also, it was amazing that there was so little separation between the bands and the audience.

I saw my first record distro at that show. Although I was afraid to look through it then, a few shows later I'd buy three 7"s from a new label out of New York called Revelation Records. I got the Gorilla Biscuits, Side by Side, and Sick of it All. A guy named Brubaker, who ran the distro, also owned a record store downtown called Chaos. About a year later, I went to a record-signing event there by Doyle and Jerry Only of the Misfits. My future high school girlfriend got her face autographed by them.

A short time later, Pizzazz got shut down after a riot ensued between the punks and Nazi skins at a Majority of One and Deadspot show that I was at. It was one of the most frightening moments of my early years. I remember a brick flying over my head—it took out a window in Majority of One's van. Revival, the other show space at the time, didn't last much longer either.

Inspired by what we experienced in Philly, Joseph and I, along with our friend, Chris, started putting on shows in south Jersey. It was around this time that I started playing music, which, through DIY touring, has taken me to over forty countries. Eventually we moved to Philly, and since there hadn't been a consistent DIY show space in the city for several years, along with some others, we decided to pick up where places like Pizzazz and Revival left off. We also wanted to incorporate some of the political aspects of the punk scene that we felt were lacking. So, we started the Cabbage Collective and invited people to table at our shows, had vegan potlucks, booked traditionally marginalized bands, sold underground books, did benefits, had picnics, and put on spoken-word shows. Every aspect of my life from where I live, to how I live, to what I eat, to where I work, has been greatly affected by the DIY punk scene. It is important to me to give back to this community, which has given so much to me. Committed for life!

T.S.O.L., MORAL MAJORITY, 5051

Scott Kelly

We all lived in North County, San Diego and had to take a series of city buses to get to downtown—one of us had done it before, so he knew the combination that got us to the show. We got out of school and began the trek. Everybody had spent the week previous getting tooled up with booze, pills, weed, etc.: we were over-prepared.

I remember when I first found out that these bands we were listening to actually played shows, and that we could go and see them: an older punk at our school had told me that he had seen Black Flag one night and I couldn't believe it. I don't know why it never occurred to me, I think that I was so overwhelmed that this music that I had been hearing in my head since I was eight was real... I felt like nothing more would come of it. Anyway, to the show…

We finally made it down there, but we ended up arriving really early. Needless to say, we were heavily loaded by the time the thing started happening. That night I remember seeing, for the first time, a number of people who would turn out to be the pillars of the scene: Mark Rude, Chris Smith, Cliff Cunningham. We made some new friends, some of which I still see today.

The early shows were much freakier than they became in the mid-80s. You had the feeling that every person there was a hardcase; there was no uniform look or way of expressing yourself, it was still to be defined. The place was small and the stage was right there in front of us. No barrier. I was momentarily stunned as I visualized seeing T.S.O.L. in this small of a venue. I think the last live band I had seen was Blue Oyster Cult so this was a whole 'nother thing entirely. They came on, and I thought they were great. A pit started and I ran out in the middle of it. Within moments, I had accidently planted my elbow in some skinhead's face, I immediately retreated into the edge of the crowd. In about a minute I felt the seas part beside me, and this guy smashed me in the side of my head. I don't know how big he was. I do know that I was about 125 lbs., and I went flying in kind of a helicopter motion to the ground. It hurt, but I was fine. A little shook up, that's for sure. I stayed away from the pit the rest of the night.

Let me pause and reflect on the gang that ran that scene. SDSH (San Diego Skinheads). We would live the next five years in fear of these guys. They were all in there thirties, big, thuggy, riding Harleys, and most of them were ex-marines. They regularly beat up kids, taxed people at parties, and brutalized anyone in their path. But somehow a number of us ended up looking to them as some sort of surrogate father figures... I guess if you get dominated long enough you become the dominator. A dark reality indeed.

Moral Majority—we knew that these guys were from our area, older brothers of some kids that we knew, they sounded really good and powerful and I remember the singer ripping out a bible and throwing it out to the crowd. I was settling down from my helicopter incident and watched from the sidelines. T.S.O.L.—when I first heard the American punk rock sound it was from a friend of mine that had made me a couple of tapes—Black Flag, Germs, Plasmatics, X, and this new band T.S.O.L. We all loved them. They had a supercharged sound, very thick and sonic. Needless to say we were very excited to be seeing them. They opened up with "Superficial Love" and the place erupted: there was a massive pit across the whole place, side to side and front to back. I was standing on a chair just watching the biggest human electric explosion that I had ever experienced. It was unfuckingbelievable. They went straight into a new song that would turn out to be "Dance With Me" (if you have it, put it on now), as they began the tribal build up at the beginning of the song something changed in the air, I didn't recognize it at the time, but I have for ever after... The feeling of riot violence overwhelmed the place and, within seconds as they broke into the main riff, the stage was taken over by SDSH. They attacked the guitarist. (There was this kid—probably ten or eleven—who sang for a band down there called the Skullbusters. He was the kid brother of one of the Skins, and had been sitting on the front of the stage. They said the guitarist kicked him.) They beat the shit out of him and broke all their gear: boots through speakers, guitars smashed, full-blown high ground take over. The cops came in and started throwing people out the door; we all made it out relatively unscathed.

Show over. I'm still close with four of the guys that I went to that first show with. I was hooked for life, the best dope you could ever find: pure human emotion.

MIST: REMEMBERING THE RAMONES

Steven Sciscenti

By the time you realize there's cancer on the skin of your nose, the game is already over and cells have been mutating by the billions. As the next step, they cut gouges out of your face, and the scars will remind you of one fact forever; before the seen and the known, the change has already happened and there isn't shit you can do about it. And so it was with the Ramones.

The problem doesn't spin back to a description of my punk years or point to the scars on my ears or to memories of slamming with abandon and trust into sweet Rene who caught me and threw me back when I was young and heartbroken and the band covered "Now I Want To Be Your Dog." That image is goofy enough for severe ridicule. The moment of punk happened more than a decade earlier. When it came I didn't recognize it for what it was, but like the cancer on my nose, everything had changed, and the '70s were already over.

But how to enter into that? I'll start with memory and move backward. In October of 2001, I sat with self-assured yuppies in an Italian restaurant in Dallas: dinner before a movie with a brilliant young ceramicist, her brother, and his programmer friends. The movie was a narrative abortion by Matthew Barney, and we had more than an hour to kill before it screened. The conversation around the meal flattened out like a white bread pancake into the distance. I ate fast and put less money than I should have next to my empty plate and got the fuck out of there and smoked cigarettes on the curb outside the theater. Karen arrived with her big goofy smile, her glasses with the duct taped bridge, and her thrift store overcoat. She sat on the curb next to me and said, "What's up?" and I said, "I fucking hate those people. Why can't I just be comfortable around normal people?" She looked at me closely and asked, "Were you ever a punk?"

There couldn't have been more than a hundred kids at the front of that stage in Milwaukee in 1977. The set was loud and repulsive and slick in the sense of something practiced down to the last nail driven into the board, with no deviation or even pauses between songs. I didn't understand what was happening, only that I knew something was. Thirty years later, I worked briefly alongside a young woman whose parents probably hadn't even fucked yet when I sat on that Wisconsin bleacher. She was the perfect Punk Rock Girl, with chopped, dyed hair and messy makeup, narrow hipbones jutting out of the front of her ragged black jeans. She wore a Ramones t-shirt so old that its holes held the thin fabric together: the real deal, probably '79 or '80. She was bright and shiny and I fell into the embarrassing move of trying to make my age impress rather than repulse her. I told her I had seen the Ramones in 1977, and her eyes grew as big as pie plates.

There are few things one can do more pathetic than pretending one is cool. The Ramones show was just the context of a moment, and I wasn't then and couldn't have been anything more than a dork with a romantic streak. The hormone infusion that kicked into my blood at fifteen was waking me up from a life of sleepwalking, and I was escaping Texas through nothing of my own doing, drifting with events as they unfolded, destroying myself and those around me as buried rage flooded me. But that came later. In the summer of 1977, I was a gentle naïf, and strange.

So this story has to begin in Texas. To be a small ethnic atheist with a crazy, violent father in suburban Texas in the 1970s was contra-indicative to mental health. Living in Richardson was like living in an abattoir, even if one's family was sane. Public school didn't help. *The bells of the schoolyard terrified me and my father's smile was like a blaze of shit* (Bukowski). I was lucky to get out alive. Or so it feels. Music didn't drive my life. '70s Top 40 radio was a filtered soundtrack drifting into a brain stuffed with cotton and barely kept alive on an I.V. of television and Hamburger Helper. My father had left for a Government job in Canada and the family sank into a trough of depression. The safety of two thousand miles of separation allowed my mother to divorce him and make plans to take herself and her children back home to Boston. We packed the old green VW bus with our travel gear and the freaked-out cat and headed north—our first destination was Milwaukee, where my Aunt Dorothy lived. Memories of the journey do not survive. But let's step back into Texas. Linger there a while. The music and the fascism can't hurt us now, right?

On our last night in Richardson, my brother and I and couple of friends broke into the empty house on Northlake Street where we sat in my old room, eerie with the ghosts of bad memory, and smoked pot for the first time, thinking ourselves cool outlaws. Passing through the park on our way back to the house from which we would leave Texas the next morning, I fell into a dream. Running, laughing through the enormous sprinklers (everything but me was big in Texas), I dove into the air and was hit by a bulb of water from the spray and it transformed into a rifle slug and I knew I'd been shot and I shouted a warning to the others to get down as I fell to the grass, an open hole in my ribcage.

Texas law in 1977 mandated that films educating children about the danger of communism—made by Senator Joseph McCarthy in 1954—be shown in ninth grade social studies classrooms throughout the state. The film was 16-millimeter, with images of the world and the Americas menaced by ominous red arrows emanating from around the curve of an animated globe. Clearly a stinking load of shit. The teacher was young and new to the school. She turned on the lights, shut down the projector, moved around to the front of her desk, leaned back against it, and asked us what we thought. Silence stretched out into the room. I don't believe any of us had ever been asked this question in school before; we had only been expected to swallow the stinking loads, not actually think about them. I now believe that her question was the most radical position she could assume in the face of Texas state laws without risking her job. I raised my hand.

I'm still not sure what possessed me. The beatings and humiliation I had received from my father had turned me into a bully's windfall and my meekness had earned me the moniker of "pussy" and "faggot" and I never spoke a word to object. She said, "Yes?" and I said the film we had just seen was a lie. I knew this as one knows the truth of one's own skin. The teacher seemed satisfied but said nothing, and did not come to my defense when, after a moment of awe, pandemonium ensued in the classroom and the children turned on me in one body and began calling me a communist. For the rest of that semester, my last in Texas until many years later, I was called "commie faggot." I new nothing of geopolitics or logic, and in my unformed mind, a suspect syllogism was formed: if it was not true that communism was bad, therefore it was good, and if THOSE kids thought being a commie faggot was bad, then that's exactly what I wanted to be. "Hey commie faggot, where you moving to—Moscow?"

The only memory that I keep from our escape from Texas was of the Wisconsin Music Festival. My older brother and I were let loose among the multiple stages of the pop compound while my mother and her sister went to hear Jazz. I was unmoved by The Spinners in their brilliant jackets, shining in the afternoon light, though they did indeed spin as they sang. We moved over to a side stage, where there were other young white kids assembling, most of them older than us. We had successfully begged my mother to shell out her threadbare clothing money to buy us each jean jackets; this was the height of cool kid fashion then and we fit right in, comfortable in our invisibility from our perch on the small bleachers at the edge of the group. A gigantic voice blared from the amp stacks, announcing that the Ramones were next up, and the small crowd exploded with joy. We'd never heard of the Ramones. Probably no one in the great state of Texas ever had, but we thought wow—this is going to be good. You could feel the anticipation in the air, and the recorded music blasting over the waiting crowd was auspicious: Supertramp's "Logical Song." How wonderful that song was to us; lush harmonies and taught staccato lyrics expressing, perfectly, the discomfort of being molded into an adult world none of us wanted anything to do with. That song sucks. But I'm not being disingenuous; in its way it was the perfect expression of the '70s, adolescent angst, and the wave of destruction that was to come with the following act.

What the young ones around me don't understand is that none of the music of the '70s was, at the time, infused with the irony with which it is understood now. It was for real, and really stupid. I can't say I knew the music was bad; I lived in a kind of passive darkness and I had no opinion either way. Small glimpses of pure light did leak their way into the Top 40 play lists—though The Kinks "Lola" and Lou Reed's "Take a Walk on the Wild Side" failed to subvert the culture or turn me into a real faggot, they were like the breath of the future fogging the windshield of pop. But Manfred Mann, Elton John and Kiki Dee, Fleetwood Mac, Electric Light Orchestra, REO Speedwagon, and The Eagles The Eagles The Eagles The Eagles The Eagles—whoops, sorry. The record skipped. Just a second here—and—oh shit, "FREEBIRD"?—saturated the airwaves over and over until masses of my synaptic connections were wasted forever. And even worse was the "Rat" music. If you ask me now I'll still tell you that anyone who thinks Led Zeppelin were great musicians either didn't have to live out the period or they have a brain the size of a pin. The "Rats" at the junior high should naturally have been my allies. These were the cool kids with the long hair, the Bad Company t-shirts and glum, cow-like looks at the back of the class, and their principle character trait was that they were as dumb as rocks. I mean that in both senses. They may have been the demographic from which punk was later to draw, but in the '70s their shit wasn't punk; it was just moronic. "Hey hey momma said the way you move gonna make you sweat gonna make you groove." My moist man hole. Hold on a second, that's my mom calling… okay, I have to give you some of this:

"You're writing a piece about the Ramones? The Ramones were so awful."

"Come on mom, when did you ever hear the Ramones?"

"Oh, I saw them when you did, at the Wisconsin Music Festival."

"You were there? I thought you were with your sister, listening to Jazz."

"Well, we were just wandering around and I was trying to find you kids. There were lots of stages and we saw you on the bleachers, so we were there when they played. They were so young… and the music was just stupid. But you didn't like them either, did you?"

"No, I didn't."

"But why are you writing about them now, then?"

"Because they're great."

"I guess I just don't get it…"

"I don't either… only a few years later I loved them, but I was there at the time and it was my first punk show and I hated it. Go figure."

> When I was young it seemed that life was so wonderful
> A miracle
> Oh it was beautiful,
> Magical
> All the birds in the trees
> Well they'd be singing so happily
> Joyfully
> Playfully
> Watching me
> "Logical Song," Supertramp, 1976

The Ramones hit the stage as the afternoon light dipped into evening. My brother and I knew that something was terribly wrong. The group was all dressed the same, which we had expected, but their uniforms were white t-shirts and jeans torn raggedly at the knee, high-top Converse sneakers, and long black hair in bangs almost touching identical black sunglasses and they were skinny and goofy and they clearly didn't give a good god damn. They were modern savages right out of the Stone Age. With no preamble, the Ramones launched into "Blitzkrieg Bop," and my brother and I felt as if we were naked at the prom. The kids at the front of the stage bopped. We sat staring with our mouths open.

> *Hey, ho, let's go*
> *Hey, ho, let's go*
> *They're forming in a straight line*
> *They're going through a tight wind*
> *The kids are losing their minds*
> *The Blitzkrieg Bop*
>   "Blitzkrieg Bop," the Ramones, 1976

I am reminded of something my old friend Mac told me. He had seen Hendrix play the Monterey Pop Music Festival in 1967. My eyes had grown as big as pie plates and I asked if he had been blown away. He said, "You have to understand. Peter, Paul and Mary were on the same bill. When Hendrix came out, no one knew what to think. What he was doing was so far ahead of the crowd nobody understood it. I don't remember him getting much applause. But everything in music changed after that."

Time is strange. I didn't tell the perfect little Punk Rock Girl that, in 1977, I hated the Ramones. No one then had any idea that punk had already broken, and a decade's time would be needed before that was clear. The Ramones could have fallen off the edge of the abyss of anonymity like so many of their contemporaries—they really weren't all that good. They were just ahead of the curve, and of course, in this they were truly great. But not even they themselves, or their most die-hard fans at the time, could have predicted their success or their meaning.

Somewhere around 1980 I became a believer, and realized that what I had seen three years earlier had been a moment never to be repeated. I did indeed become a Communist and did my level best to be a faggot. When punk broke into my consciousness I was ready for it, but in fact it was already a done deal. The mutation had spread before any of us were truly aware of it, and the moment was over. I'm not saying that the bands that have worked since are not sincere or important, only that between the inception of punk and its realization lay a crucial gap of understanding. Later, reaching out to it was like trying to touch mist rising above my hand into the trees. *When I was young, it seemed that life was so wonderful...*

TELL ME WHO HAS WON WHEN NOTHING REMAINS?

Rob Fish

I grew up in Edison, NJ, which is a suburb about forty-five minutes from New York City. I was rather oblivious to music when I was growing up. Besides seeing how a Janis Joplin song could bring my mother to tears, to me, music seemed removed from life. In 1981, when I was nine years old, a kid moved to my neighborhood from Spanish Harlem. He and his older brother brought my first glimpse of hip-hop music. Although the social environment I was growing up in was very different from those of the early hip-hop artists, I was enamored by the realism and urgency of their music. To this day, one listen to "The Message" by Grand Master Flash and the Furious Five illustrates, to me, the power that music can possess. Over the next few years, I dove into hip-hop music and its subculture. By the eighth grade I started to get into skateboarding and dabbled in punk music.

When I got into high school I found a whole scene of skateboarders and my transition from hip-hop to punk started. On the first day of school I ran into a kid I knew years before and we talked about music. I was into hip-hop and he was into heavy metal, but we bonded over our passion for music. As our class ended, he handed me a tape that changed my life. It was the first Black Flag EPs; from then on, I was hooked into punk. Within the scene of skateboarders at our school, there was a smaller group of kids whose passion for skateboarding was dwarfed by that of punk, and those were the kids I became close to.

The problem was that we were between the ages of thirteen and fifteen, and had no way to venture down to City Gardens, which was the big NJ punk club, or to CBGB's in NYC which—although just a train ride away—had an age requirement of sixteen and older. The best we could manage was trips to New Brunswick, to the two music stores that carried lots of punk records and hosted afternoon bands, to quench our thirst for punk music.

On one of our many trips to New Brunswick, to skateboard and hit the record store, we found a flier for a Corrosion of Conformity show. The show was at Middlesex County College, which is located in Edison, NJ. We were stunned and excited—in disbelief—a punk show was coming to us. I believe the bill was Token Entry, 76% Uncertain, and Corrosion of Conformity.

I remember the nervous anticipation for my first show. Although the music wasn't new to me, I had spent the last year imagining what a show would be like. My frame of reference was the kids I knew, and the pictures, lyrics, and energy of the records. I remember skating to the show with friends and how excited we were. I can't help but laugh at how cool we tried to play it. When we got to the show, we were surrounded by older kids who were not as I expected, at least not in my imagination. They were all friendly and rather un-intimidating. When the bands played I was in awe of the sight of the pit and stage-diving.

I remember the nervous feeling when I walked by Corrosion of Conformity's merch table because there *they* were. My friends and I listened to their records all the time and the energy, the anger...it was beyond anything we had experienced first hand. It was surreal to see these guys. I remember watching Ari buy a pair of Corrosion of Conformity boxer shorts! Fucking bastard. I did manage to get the "Tell me who has won when nothing remains" t-shirt, which I kept as a treasure for over thirteen years, until it got ripped completely off of me at a 108 show in Poland.

When Corrosion of Conformity played I was totally blown away. The intensity of not just the band, but also the environment was so powerful. For fleeting moments I would get lost in the energy and the moment, and that left a very powerful impression on me.

Within the next year, we ventured to CBGB's with our nifty fake IDs, and we found a slightly scarier scene, at least externally... But once everyone was inside and the first chord was played, the energy and emotion was something I could never forget.

Over the years, it is almost like I have come back to the limitations of my first show. Maybe it is the natural effect of attending and playing shows for the last twenty-one years that hinders my ability to relish every chord, but it is still an unbelievable feeling when the power of the music, the energy of the kids, and the purpose of punk music hits you so hard that you lose yourself to the moment.

DESCENDENTS '85

DAVID BOISINEAU

Fall of '85. I don't know what month, just that it was the Fall. I was in the sixth grade and eleven years old at the time. I got home from school one day, ran in the house to grab my board to go skate, and my big brother Joey comes down from upstairs and says, "Hey, the Descendents are playing tonight, do you want to go?" I said yeah, but that I had to ask mom. Joey said he already had and it was cool. See, Joey was nine years older than me and had been playing in hardcore bands in Richmond, VA since the time he was fourteen years old. My parents were cool and trusted my brother to take care of him and me. So I dropped off my bookbag and left with my brother. Going with him to a show, or anywhere for that matter, was cool 'cause he had this truck with skate/band stickers on it, and he always listened to punk rock LOUD. Growing up in the lily-white suburbs, this stuck out. We stopped by his ex-band mate's house (I own the house across the street from their old house now, twenty years later). They were in a band called Sordid Doktrine and they were one of the opening bands that night. Anyway, we got to the show way early; Joey knew the guys at the club so we got in free.

The Descendents were sound checkin' and I had NO idea what was going on. I need to say at this point, that two nights ago I was at CBGB's for one of the "last" shows of that great club, to see Avail and Bad Brains. There was a kid in the front row that had a shirt and ball cap on that he had drawn band names and straight edge logos all over. My buddy was making fun of this kid when I thought of my sweatshirt at the Decsendents show—Blaze orange zip up hoodie that I had drawn MILO and the words "Sour Grapes" on the back of. Yeah, it wasn't a very "cool guy" thing to do. Anyway, it was cold in the club, The Pyramid, which was a gay dance club on the weekends and had shows during the week. Guys were lingering around a space heater and I overheard a couple of 'em having a conversation about 8-track tapes; it was Bill Stevenson, but I had no idea at the time. Even if you had told me his name I wouldn't have known, I just knew I liked the Descendents' music.

In the back of the club was a little diner. In between opening bands there were TVs in that diner with some band's video playing. It was GWAR. I had no idea what it was all about; I just thought it was kind of weird.

The show finally started and the Decsendents came on stage. It was the *ALL* record tour, so Milo had this wooden podium and the first song was the "ALL-O-GISTICS." He was swinging and swaying all over, preaching that song. Then BAM! DECSENDENTS! Stevenson had on C.O.C. boxer shorts and no britches, with extra sticks stuck in the waistband. Milo was very, uh, in your face. Bug was there too, managing the stage, and if I remember, correctly Alvarez was on that tour.

I had never been part of something like that, but wanted to be right up in the mix! Keep in mind that I was eleven, and I was very small compared to most everyone else. But I got up front. I got moshed on and shredded. At some point I moved to the safety of the side of the stage, and got out of the mix. I don't think that I once got tired or bored with them playing that night. It was lost upon me what I was witnessing. I would get to see them only once more that spring and then never again. It started something that would keep with me from eleven years old up till now, even though I'm in my thirties, wear cowboy boots not Vans, and listen to country music.

A BOY BECOMES HUMAN: MY FIRST TIME

John Poddy

Like most disaffected youth who grew up in the Southern California suburbs (Mission Viejo), I knew there had to be more out there then the excessive '70s arena rock and the "take it easy" sound that was prevalent in the LA area. I had tended to gravitate to the glam rock of England such as Bowie, T-rex, Sweet, Eno, etc., as well as stateside clown-rockers KISS. A typical middle-70s family weekend activity in the Poddy household included a healthy dose of television. Like many other American households, on Fridays, we would watch the Brady's, the Partridge's, and the "risqué" *Love American Style*, but then we would stay up late to watch Burt Sugarman's *Midnight Special*. Saturday nights would center around whatever crappy *Barnaby Jones/Columbo* was on, then we would watch *Saturday Night Live* and *Don Kirshner's Rock Concert*. These late night shows gave the young John Poddy my first views of artists including the great David Bowie, Blondie, Patti Smith, Talking Heads, Elvis Costello, the B-52's, and Devo. Magazines such as *Circus, Creem,* and *Hit Parader* would give me—in between the Nugent, Aerosmith, Zeppelin, Van Halen onslaught—access to the Pistols, Iggy, Ramones, and other punk snippets. By junior high, I had started accumulating a pretty impressive record collection. I loved the rock and roll. But something was missing. The live show. For years, I eagerly awaited the Sunday edition of the *Los Angeles Times* so that I could read the Calendar section, where they would have all the advertisements for the upcoming rock shows. I would lovingly rub my fingers over them, fantasizing about going to see these exciting, mysterious gods, the legends of the 8-track, live in-person. Oh how a young teen boy could only hope and dream.

The neighborhood kids went to see KISS at the Anaheim Stadium show. It was the tour for the *Destroyer* album. Being the little nerdy freak kid with the glasses, I wasn't invited. By this time, not being included with the locals was old hat so I wasn't surprised that I wasn't invited, but I still wish I could have gone and seen Ace Frehley shoot fireworks out of his smoking Les Paul. Oh Yeah. Gibson guitars and Pearl drums because they only used the best. That is, until Ibanez offered Paul Stanley some bucks to put his name on that Iceman guitar. I never did see the original incarnation of KISS. I saw them during the '80s, at one point, after they had taken their makeup off. I'm not even sure which album it was. Standard rock show. I thought I was over it, but when I saw them in 1998 for the "Psycho Circus" tour, I cried when Ace Frehley sang his two songs. By this time I had been to hundreds of shows of all shapes and sizes, and one thing (of many) I know is that Gene Simmons and Paul Stanley ripped off millions of KISS fans when they limited the Ace Frehley vocal contribution to the band. When it comes to rock stars, Ace is the real deal. His solo album was clearly the best, AND I finally got the sunburst Les Paul so I could be just like him.

But enough about KISS, this is about punk rock. Or is KISS punk rock? The "serious" musicians hated them. Often times they were called things along the lines of a cartoon joke band. I remember when *Guitar Player* put Ace on the cover. The next issue had subscription cancellation letters galore. They did what they wanted. Isn't that punk? They were also the first band on their label, Casablanca, which some might call an indie—maybe until the Donna Summer and Village People stuff came out on it. Regardless, they weren't my first show.

My first rock show, and this is debatable, was *Beatlemania* at the Shubert Theater. Was it a rock show or a Broadway style production? I went to this show with my mom and probably others, although I can't remember whom. I was in the sixth or seventh grade, and at this time, preferred my bands to wear glitter, big shoes, and make-up, so I wasn't really aware of the significance of the Beatles in rock history. Having broken up when I was five, it didn't have much impact on me. I figured it out later though. Maybe the Beatles were the first punk band? After all, they were more popular than Jesus. The *Beatlemania* show did have films prior to the actual music. But so did Devo and the Butthole Surfers—bands I saw later on. But *Beatlemania* was really the first show that I went to where they had guitars amps and drums. Sure the "Paul" played right handed, but who cares, it was loud. But, as everyone knows, in December of 1979 we were all informed that "phony Beatlemania had bitten the dust." If Joe Strummer says it's a scam, who am I to argue?

So on we continue. It's now 1979 and I still have yet to see original rock music. I continue my weekly ritual with the Calendar section and now I am working a part time job at Shakey's Pizza for $2.50 an hour, when I see an add for Foreigner who is touring to promote the *Double Vision* album. Young John Poddy gets excited and along with my friend Mostafa, we convince his aunt Mickey to take us to the Forum, in Inglewood, to see the show. This was the same forum where the Los Angeles Lakers played, and at that time was just referred to as the Fabulous Forum, prior to becoming the Great Western (after the bank) Forum—which was kind of the beginning of Sports Arenas/Concert venues whoring themselves out for naming rights. It's actually kind of funny that an Arena built for and primarily used for the hyper-masculine world of professional sports would be referred to as "fabulous." Anyway... Mostafa's aunt had taken him to see KISS for the "Alive II" tour just the previous year. Unfortunately that was before I knew him, so young Poddy got assed out on that one by a mere few months. Tickets for the Foreigner show were $6.75, $7.75, and $8.75—a lot of money at the time, so we went with the $6.75 level. We didn't buy Mickey's ticket or chip in for gas (some might consider that action itself to be kind of punk thus making this my first punk show, but I'm not going to go there). Looking back on it, we should have ponied up some compensation funds, and later on I felt bad about it, but we didn't. I have a history of blundering socially and this was just one event after previous blunders and a precursor to many to come. The show itself was good. It was a slick well-produced major-label band gig. The opener was the Walter Egan Band who had a hit song "Magnet and Steel," which got some revival in the movie *Boogie Nights*. Foreigner rattled off the hits of their first two albums, did the requisite encores, and even whipped out the dry ice machines for the extended flute solo in the song "Starrider." The overall experience was all right, but there was a sense that there was something better out there.

My next foray was later that year. I convince my dear mother that since she had taken my older sister to see America (you know, the horse with no name/muskrat love band), it was her duty as a parent to not show favoritism, and I was entitled to my trip to the land of rock. Now keep in mind that if Southern California had any kind of decent public transport, I probably would have found my way to the shows myself. Yet even now, twenty-seven years later, they still can't figure it out so Ma Poddy got to chaperone. For this one I chose the delightful combo bill

of Sammy Hagar, el rocker rojo, and the slowest moving AOR band ever,
Boston. "What's with the hippies Pod?" one might ask. I couldn't tell you.
So, along with my brother Mike, we went off to the Forum with Mom
for a night of rocking. The seats we had that night (again the cheapest
money could buy, although Mom was a bit more savvy than Mickey and
made us buy her ticket up front) were next-to-back row on the side of
the arena. Now when you sit on the side of the Forum for a basketball
game, you had a prime half-court seat. For a concert, you're in the sky
and off to the side. So we're sitting there with Mom, in the top of the
Forum, it's 1979, and the second the lights go out, it seemed like every
hippie in the place (God Bless em) sparked a doob. Within moments we
were in a hazy cloud of THC. And we got high. This was the only time
in my life that I ever got a true contact high. Then Sammy Hagar puts on
the most rockin' show in the history of rock, using the F-word in every
cliché rock and roll line that he spewed out. This, of course, titillated the
eleven- and fifteen-year-old boys in our party, but not the forty-year-
old woman who was with us. After Hagar played his particular brand of
screaming manboy rock, Boston, much like Foreigner, put on a slick, well-
produced show, which ran through the hits of their first two albums.
The funniest moment of the night was on the drive home, when Mom
took us on this elaborate detour through Lakewood so that we could
go to this 24-hour donut shop that she knew of from when she grew up
in that area. Mom had the munchies, tee hee hee. For years my brother
and I used to laugh about how Mom got high and never even knew. Then
in the early-90s, we were all in Flagstaff for my sister's wedding, and we
are at this bar, and we're all drinking and the discussion gets around
to the legalization of drugs. Mom, of course, puts in her two cents and
I respond with, "How would you know? You've never been high." And
without missing a beat Mom shoots back with, "Yes, I have. At that damn
Sammy Hagar concert you dragged me to!!!" I guess the joke was on us.

Finally comes 1980, and John Poddy gets a license. I had my copy of
X's *Los Angeles* which was making the regular rotation on my turntable
(record player in those days), when lo and behold, in my beloved calendar section is an advertisement for an X show at some place in Hollywood called the Starwood. Of course, having only had my license for a
short while, my parents weren't about to let me drive to Hollywood, so I
use the old standby, and say I am going to a friend's house. I am not really
sure whom I went to the show with and I don't remember how I figured

out the directions to the venue, but I can still remember the drive. Going through the mini-tunnel on the Hollywood freeway that opens up onto the view of the LA skyline, the people lining the streets of Santa Monica Blvd, so alive with energy that it masked the desperation of the people lining the street—a desperation that one is immune to in the suburbs.

We found street parking and made our way to the club. Our Shawn Cassidy hairstyles and Op clothes are in contrast to the leather clothes, combat boots, Germs logo'd army jackets, trench coats, and cut and dyed hair that was the more prevalent look among the other attendees. Amazingly, no one gave us any grief for looking different, which was something I saw a lot of later. I can remember waiting in line, and a car was backing into one of the, maybe, ten parking spaces. The locals were helping out by indicating, with hand gestures, to continue backing up. They kept signaling until the car slammed into the wall of the club. I thought this to be the funniest, most irreverent act I had ever seen. Punk, if you will.

Finally the doors open, we pay our $5 and gain admittance to the temple that is the Starwood, which may be more famous for being owned by organized crime figure Eddie Nash, who was connected to the Laurel Canyon Murders, which involved porn king John Holmes. But this night it belonged to John Poddy: young, fresh, and eager for a new experience. We went in and I was amazed that I could walk right up to the stage. I could almost touch the drums and amplifiers. It was a view that was unobtainable to me at the Forum shows. The Starwood was so full of energy that I knew something good was going to happen. I had specifically gone to see X, but the opening band was Vancouver, Canada's D.O.A. I had not heard of D.O.A. then, but when they came down the stairs that led to the stage, plugged in their guitars, and hitched up to the drums, this band just exploded. It was like getting hit in the face, but in a good way. This was what I was waiting for. This was real. This was high-energy rock and roll. I could see the sweat on their faces as they tore up the stage. I could see the spittle fly from their mouths as they shouted through the tunes. I was physically swept up in the movement of the crowd. There was a "pit," but it was years before they called it "moshing," and it wasn't violent. You didn't feel like you were in danger of getting hurt. If you fell there was a hand to pick you up. It wasn't that way by the time I graduated high school. This Starwood show was the classic D.O.A.

line-up, with Chuck Biscuits (pre-Black Flag, Circle Jerks, Danzig, Social D) and Randy Rampage (pre-solo rock star and Annihilator) that went on to record the required *Hardcore 81* album. The impact on a young John Poddy was phenomenal. Cut time, machine gun drumming behind pulsing bass, and distorted bar chords went through my skin and imbedded into my torso. This was truly the night I was born. After D.O.A. was X. Having just released their definitive punk album *Los Angeles*, X was fresh and energetic as well. They played all the songs off the album, so I was familiar with what I heard. I specifically remember the absence of the Ray Manzarek keyboards on the song "Nausea" and thinking that it was better without them. Chunk chunk chunk chunk chunk chunk chunk chunk. Two awesome indie punk bands, what more could one ask for? But then it gets better. At that time, LA Clubs often would only book two bands and then have two shows, one at 8 o'clock and one at 10 or 10:30. If you were at the first show, you just stayed for the second show AND you weren't required to pay a cover for that second show. So not only did I get to see D.O.A. and X for my first punk show, I got to see them twice!!! An addict was created that night. I went to every show I could at clubs as well known as the Whiskey, Roxy, The Country Club, Cuckoo's Nest etc... To big punk shows at the Olympic and Santa Monica Civic, to little shithole clubs that didn't last two shows. I saw bands ranging from PIL to Dead Kennedys to Black Flag to 999 and everything in-between. Driving home from the Starwood that night, I decided that it was a requirement that I start a band, and I did. I have played hundreds of shows and continue to do so to this day. I plan to do so until I die.

Has the "scene" changed? Of course it has. Is it better or worse? Who's to say? I can only hope that every day, boys and girls around the world will walk into a club and experience the feelings and energy that I felt back in 1980. That day had such an impact on the person I am today.

THOUGHTS OF YESTERDAY

Shawna Kenney

We are going to our first show. Not one like the barn bash we had at Margie's farm on Halloween, or the ones the Roadside Petz have played at the dumb Teen Scene, but a real one at a real club in DC, seeing a real band on tour all the way from California: T.S.O.L.—the True Sounds of Liberty. They are not my favorite, but Josh's dad bought him tickets and said he would drive us and Josh could take five friends. I am the only girl, but I am always the only girl when we skate or watch skate videos or tape records at each other's houses. His dad is cool—he's a librarian at the college and plays Pink Floyd on the living room stereo. There is no music in my house, except for my small record collection. On the night of the show, Josh's dad picks me up in his mini-van. Josh is sitting in front, his hair all done up. He is the only kid in our little Maryland town with a full-on mohawk. Toby says he's got the perfect skull for it. Josh's head is pretty perfectly shaped, and the newly shaved parts are just a little lighter than the smooth olive skin of his face.

"How'd you get it to stand up?" I ask, getting in the van.

"Knox-Blox," he says, smiling.

"Huh?"

"Gelatin," he explains.

"Oh. Cool."

Mike Baillie is next—he lives on the way out of town. I have heard so much about this kid, how cool he is. Josh always says his full name because there are three other Mikes we hang out with. This one goes to Josh's high school. Toby and Todd go to the other public school. I go to a private Catholic one, which I hate. Even with my scholarship it still costs my parents a lot of money—they make monthly payments. I tell them they could save so much if they just let me go to public, but no matter how much I beg, they won't let me change. We all skate together at Trevor's ramp or in the Square—our town's version of a mall—on the weekends. If there's really nothing else to do we go to parties or a foot-ball game once in awhile, but in packs, because the jocks sometimes beat up on punks. Rob is a star quarterback at Josh's school, but he's a skater too, so we don't hate him.

We pull up to a little white house and a tall, lanky kid with baboon-like long arms comes out and gets in and sits behind me.

"Mike, Shawna. Shawna, Mike," Josh says.

"S'up," says Mike from under an army-green skull-cap. His huge brown eyes are half-shut. He lays his head against the van window and falls asleep before we're out of his driveway.

"Are you ok? Are you sick?" I ask back to Mike. He shakes his head no, eyes still closed.

"Duuuude, Mike Baillie's always tired," Josh shrugs.

He pops in a tape of the band we're about to see and sings along.

"Superficial love! Only for a FUCK!" he yells, shaking a fist in the air from under his denim jacket. His Dad doesn't seem to mind. Josh spits out all the lyrics the whole way there, and I stare out the window and sometimes back at the Mike Baillie kid.

When we get to the 9:30 Club, we park around the corner near a store with a sign that says "XXX Videos." We joke that it means "straight edge," but we know it doesn't. Outside of the club Josh's dad gives us each a ticket, and we walk through graffitied glass doors and get in line in a long, dark hallway. I am trying not to stare, but everyone looks so cool—so much older than us—except Josh's dad, with his dark beard and brown leather jacket...he looks like a dad. When we get inside, my eyes drink in everything around us—the walls are painted thick with black, a pole sits in the middle of the dance floor, also painted black, with a chair attached up high, where an employee sits perched with a video camera. A narrow shelf of a few inches juts out of the back of the room—a perfect viewing spot for short people like me, but with only enough room for two or three, without touching. A pretty red-haired chick who looks like Siouxsie Sioux tends the bar, jumping up on it from time to time to catch the action. There's another bar down the short hall and in the back, but it's dark, with barstools for the hardcore—those who aren't there to watch bands, those who are drowning out the cherry blossoms and tourists outside in their own way. Fourteen steep stairs lead me down to the bathrooms, women's on the right, men's on the left, but who cares, really? People go wherever they want here. Both smell like puke. The girls' room walls say things like ME & JANINE ARE LESBOS or STIV BATORS HAS A FAT COCK. Two doors are missing from the three stalls. Back out and down the hall is a $1 coat check, but who uses it? It's a place to get away from the bad opening bands and talk to the coat-check girl, who wears a black leather motorcycle jacket with a pink Hello Kitty painted on the back.

When the last opening band finishes, we smush ourselves against the stage. Josh's dad is in the back, drinking a beer. The band comes out, tunes their guitars, and launches right into their first song. It is distorted and perfect. The noise from their amps melts that whole other world away faster than nuclear weapons, better than drugs. Josh is singing toward the singer and so is everybody, even Mike Baillie. Someone runs on-stage and dives into the center of the crowd. Someone elbows me hard in the boob—an accident, I'm sure—but it hurts, so I drift to the back and stand with Josh's dad.

"Can I get you a Coke?" he asks.

I nod, wondering how much sodas are at a nightclub. He brings me back a big plastic cup filled with ice and sugary goodness.

"How much do I owe you?" I ask. He shakes his head and smiles.

"Don't worry about it, honey."

After the show we ride back, smelling like smoke and sweat, talking about every little move the band made, and those skinheads.

"That big one was standing next to me the whole time," says Josh. "He was staring at my 'Nazi punks fuck off' pin, but he didn't say anything."

"I heard their new thing is they stand next to you, line up their feet next to yours, and beat you up and take your Doc Martens," says Toby. "This guy in the bathroom told me that Lefty, that big black girl, is a skinhead and she beat him up once."

"Get the fuck outta here," says Josh. "She's black."

"I know," says Toby. "But she's still a skin-chick and she's huge!"

"How does that work?" I ask. "Being a black skinhead?"

"Maybe she's racist against white people?" Mike Baillie says.

"But she was hanging with those white power skins in the back," says Toby. "They had red laces in their boots and that means they're white power," he adds.

"Maybe she's just weird and likes to fuck with people," says Josh.

We all agree that's probably it. We have another hour before we're home, but it's a school-night, and the deal was that we'd all go to school the next day, so we fall asleep, one-by-one, leaving Josh's dad with Pink Floyd blasting to the windy highway.

We get to Josh's at 3 am. His mom has laid out sleeping bags for everyone all over the living room, and a cot upstairs in Josh's room for me. His Dad will drop me off at school in the morning on his way to work. We all agree to wear our t-shirts, but I know I can't because of the dress code. All shirts must have a collar. No denim jackets or pants. And ladies must wear socks or stockings. Which isn't as bad as uniforms, but severely limits my outfits. The only thing I can mess with is my hair. I shave, dye, and bleach it as much as I can. I pierce my left ear three times. The nuns can't give me demerits for these things.

"Who's going to Baltimore for G.I.'s and the Descendents at the Loft next week?" Josh asks everyone at breakfast the next morning. We all nod while eating our cereal, silently wondering if his dad will drive us again, or how we'll get to the city-that's-an-hour-away.

"I'm getting my license this weekend," I say. "I'll drive."

"What if you fail?" someone asks.

"I won't."

I do pass, and life begins.

BLITZ / NO SUPPORT / RENWICK BATS / IRONING BOARDS

Sean McGhee

The exact date is lost in time, although possibly it doesn't matter; it was definitely February 1979, and the concert (this was before I'd become hip to rock slang to call them "gigs") was at Mick's Club, Fisher Street, Carlisle.

Those who appeared were all local Carlisle and Cumbria bands: Blitz from Aspatria; Renwick Bats from Penrith; No Support and local punk heroes, The Ironing Boards, both from Carlisle.

I was still at school, and was one of those lucky kids who came across a teacher that not only appreciated punk, but had actually been checking out bands at the Roxy in London throughout 1977. I think I managed to get a lift to his house courtesy of my Dad, who at the time wasn't exactly enamored to punk or my early experimentation in punk-style dress, but he was always willing to drive me places. I arrived there and with a motley crew of young local punks from West Cumbria, we piled into the back of Paul (Burdus)'s knackered little van to power our way through the truly windy back roads of rural north Cumbria until we arrived in cold, damp Carlisle. Exiting from the van, we traipsed single file down the then crumbling, decrepit, Victorian un-splendour of the badly lit Fisher Street, searching for "Mick's Club" (owned and operated by Mick Potts of Cumbria's very own Gateway Jazz Band).

Situated below street level, the basement venue was entered via a set of concrete steps. Inside I got my first real taste of the punk rock experience—loud, punk disco, playing period-punk Dead Boys, Ramones, Clash...hell, even Blondie! There were lots of people standing or sitting around trying to look vacant or faintly aggressive or both. The venue was a dimly lit, smoky, and crowded jazz bar, with little tables complete with checked tablecloths and, most bizarre of all, a great big (real) fire by the bar, adding a surreal edge and extra heat to an already hot club.

I was too young for drinking, and back then the taste put me off anyway, so I tried unsuccessfully to get as near to the front as possible when Blitz began. Through the haze of time I remember they looked sharp and punky in all leather jackets, tight trousers, and zips. For a three-piece they kicked out an agreeable racket that culminated in their anthem "Baseball Boots," and a skewed re-visit to Elvis' "Blue Suede Shoes." Next up was a Carlisle band called No Support, all longhair, flares, and post-punk left-field noise. They weren't cool or punky enough for my youthful biased eyes, but their front man Chris Robson was destined to go on to be a mainstay of the early Carlisle and Cumbrian punk scene via his record label Matchbox Classics and fanzine *Monkey Talk*.

From the rural outpost of Penrith (home constituency then to ex-UK Home Secretary Willie Whitelaw), The Renwick Bats looked cool and sounded great. Appearing like a ragged cross between the Small Faces and The Bay City Rollers, they all wore spiky feather cuts and homemade punk styles. They even had their own theme song, "Do The Bat," and dance, "The Penrith Worm" (named after a mythical medieval creature that terrorized the good people of said town). Other numbers like "Suicide" and "No Direction" had me hooked. The Renwick Bats were appealing and loads of fun. A few months later I would debut with my own band supporting The Bats, but I digress…

Closing the evening was, in my eyes, the epitome of cool, punk sophistication. All gob and cocky attitude, The Ironing Boards were two parts art school and one part street thug.

Their music was tight, effective, and largely covers, but I thought they were great. "Sonic Reducer," "New Rose," Ramones numbers, and a smattering of their own songs. Leering at the audience with a detached interest and enjoying a spitting duel with the front row of manic dancers, their front man, bedecked in a woman's fake leopard skin coat, looked every inch the first wave punk cliché.

They finished with a cover of Black Sabbath's "Paranoid" (The Dickies had just released their version) that caused my punk rock art teacher real consternation. "Punk was about destroying shit like that," he proclaimed. It took me years to understand his point entirely, but I still love the song.

BERKELEY IS MY BABY

Paul Curran

My first punk show was the Dead Kennedys, the Pop-O-Pies, and Pariah at the Keystone Berkeley, in late-1983. I wish I knew the exact date of this show. At the time, I lived with my mom in the sleepy hamlet of Benicia and my dad lived in Berkeley. As is typical with weekend parents, he let me do whatever I wanted. Not only that, but he pretty much encouraged me to be a punk rocker. When I was eight years old he took me to see the weekly midnight showing of *Rocky Horror Picture Show* at the UC Theatre, just a block away from the Keystone. It was there that I discovered counter-culture, which became the most exciting thing in the world to me. Being into *Rocky Horror* and the B-52's, I felt so much more worldly and enlightened than anyone else in my hometown, and I would get a sense of satisfaction at being called "weird" by the kids at school. Looking back, I think that people weren't as much hostile as they were confused. Kids didn't understand transvestitism, new wave, or punk rock enough to hate it. So for the most part I was just regarded as a kid with unusual interests. And, fortunately, I had supportive parents who, rather than sending me to an institution, were happy to see me getting interested in music and politics. So, of course, my dad had no issues with dropping his thirteen-year-old son off at the hardcore punk show for the evening...

My memory is pretty shitty, but here's what I do remember about the Keystone: It was pretty big for a punk venue, but not huge—a little bigger than Gilman. It was kinda dirty, with flyers on the walls. There were only a few dozen people when I got there, which eventually grew to a few hundred. Not too many people looked like my idea of "crazy punkers," and the vibe was pretty friendly.

The sound system was blaring some awesome music that I had never heard before, and I particularly liked this one song where the chorus just repeated "fuck you." That was the Avengers, of course. A fact I learned just by asking a random dude at the show. Thanks, random dude, for not spitting on me and calling me a poser!

The Pop-O-Pies were a weird band that everyone just yelled at the whole time they were playing. People kept shouting, "Truckin'!" but I didn't know why. They only played a few songs, one of which was about fifteen minutes long and had one repeating chord and one repeating line of lyrics that went, "Make those donuts with extra grease, this one is for the chief of police." Years later I got a hold of the first Pop-O-Pies record and was finally able to appreciate the genius of this band.

While Pariah and Pop-O-Pies played, I saw that some people were sitting on the stage, off to the side, where you could watch the band without getting smashed against the stage or moshed by people "thrashing." Before the DKs came on I timidly crawled up on stage and squatted in a corner against the stage left wall, where I was sure that someone was going to tell me to shove off—or maybe even just shove me off—but it didn't happen. I watched *from the stage* as the most exciting band of the day ripped through their set. It's hard to remember or imagine how I must have looked while this was going on. Scared? Ecstatic? Dumbfounded? I do know that from then on I considered myself a "punk" instead of just someone who was into punk music. It was my initiation, even though no one but me was there to acknowledge it.

What I knew about the punk scene before that was what I had read: the violent world of Black Flag and Sex Pistols shows. The punk scene that I found was accepting, and even welcoming, to all kinds of people—no matter how tough or "punk" you looked. Punk rock was only scary in the nervous excitement sense. Later, I lost my naïveté and learned that there were plenty of people in the punk scene that you should be afraid of, but by that time I also had friends to stick with at the shows and I've never really felt unsafe.

NEUROSIS, STIKKY, SLAMBODIANS, PLAID RETINA, SKIN FLUTES

Craigums

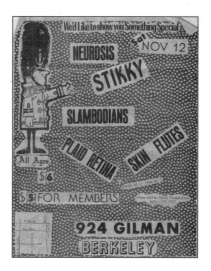

I had seen bands before in backyards and garages and junior high school quads, and my folks of course took me to some proper "rock shows." (1984 was a particularly good year for that—RATT, Weird Al, Huey Lewis & the News…) But my first official punk show—the first show I attended that did more than just deafen me—was this one.

I was a high school sophomore. I had a blond mohawk that easily doubled as a surfer/skater cut and seemed requisite for anyone with a Gotcha t-shirt, a pair of Vans hi-tops, and a BMX bike with pegs on the hubs. On occasion, when The Cure or Depeche Mode came to town, my hair was dyed black and teased, but usually it just hung in my eyes like limp, moldy hay. I spent four to five hours a day riding my BMX bike, so in my small town I wasn't too removed from the skaters. They always had the best music to ride to, plus they were always the first ones to find new ditches to ride and cover in spray paint and have unprotected teenage sex in.

Truth be told, I'm pretty sure all the punkers in my town thought I was a poser. For a thirteen-year-old with varying influences, I couldn't make up my mind between being a goth kid or a BMX rat or a valley punk. I remember the senior class president had a leather jacket with a Misfits crimson ghost mural on the back. He used to walk behind me in the halls singing "It's hip to be queer." Instead of cowering, I would usually play up the part just to annoy him (and others like him), till eventually nobody but the metalheads continued to pick on me.

So between hanging out with the skaters and the leather-jacketed, spiky-haired, get-drunk-by-the-train-tracks punkers, I was eventually led closer and closer to true underground music. Lots of boombox-to-boombox taping followed, and weekly we'd hit up the local coke-front of a record store. *BAM*, a local free rag, always listed bands with intriguing names (Millions of Dead Cops, Mr. T Experience, Yeastie Girlz, Crummy Musicians, etc.), playing at a place called "924 Gilman St" in Berkeley.

Inevitably, the moment one of my friends got access to a car (not a license, just a car) we set out to find Gilman St. We got unbelievably lost and missed most of the Skin Flutes, but there was still plenty to marvel at. The club itself provided everything you knew your parents wouldn't approve of—it was in a bad neighborhood where kids with mohawks and spikes on their clothes were drinking and fucking in the bushes. From inside blared loud, aggressive, obnoxious music performed by kids not much older than me.

I remember buying the Plaid Retina record before they even played just because I was excited I could actually walk right up and talk to a bona fide touring band. They were from Fresno, and I thought they were big shit because they had traveled all the way up to Berkeley to play a show. When they actually performed I was floored. If memory serves, their guitar player used two cabinets on either side of the stage to project stereo images of his crazy-assed guitar parts, and he layered them all over some twisted bass/drum grooves. This was at the early stages of the Bay Area funk/punk scene and this band borrowed many of those elements, but fused them in such un-inimitable, inaccessible way that I was dumbfounded. I still listen to that 7".

The Slambodians were exactly what my suburban, out-of-touch, only-know-what-I-read-about-in-*Thrasher*-and-watched-in-videos imagination had expected. The drummer, who played hyper-fast beats, seemed to be struggling with all his might not to lose it. I distinctly remember him playing so hard he looked both terrified and on the verge of tears. (FYI, he is now the drummer for Mr. T Experience.) A bass player and a guitar player, who alternated, accompanied him between punk rock and Anthrax-ish mosh parts. It was absolutely frantic and I jumped in the slampit with both boots. The singer was so intense and aggressive that I feared I would get punched in the face for no reason other than because I was paying attention. (Incidentally, this did happen some months later at a pizza place in Redwood City, and I still have the extra cartilage on the inside of my lip to show for it.)

Between bands, a sticker was handed to me that read "Free Tampons Or Bloodshed." *Man, that blew my mind…* It was such a loaded statement—gender equality, political health issues, shock and gore, and all on a red photocopied paper sticker—punk rock in its purest form.

Stikky turned out to be the band I would have been in if I had a clue. They were as fast and intense as they were irreverent and goofy. (We would later play Chris Dodge's wedding reception on the same stage—which was like the biggest honor ever, especially since Stikky played too.) They made homemade cassettes featuring like fifty songs and sold them for a dollar—how could I not like them?!

I remember a guy named Tony having a seizure in the middle of the floor. Nobody seemed to mind. A few minutes later he did it again on the stage and again, nobody seemed to care. I saw him at show after show for years, having seizures whenever the mood struck him. They weren't health-related seizures like I had suspected, but rather his way of "expressing himself." Gilman punks were wise to him, but when Tony would pull this stunt at The Stone or The Omni, people not in-the-know freaked out, which was probably how he wanted it. Tony was the first person I ever met where I thought "that man is going to die an unnatural death well before his time." He was always incoherently drunk and causing trouble, and he looked like a crime scene, all dirtied and disheveled and often a little bloody. A couple years later he simply vanished and I thought for sure he had been hit by a train or killed by skinheads. Ten years later I was shocked to see that not only was he still alive (and looking exactly like he did the day he vanished), but also together enough to front a band called STFU. Go figure…

Neurosis looked the most like I wanted a punk band to look—unkempt, scary, and dangerous—but they played too slow. Mid-tempo music seemed too metal, and I was coming to a point where aggressive music had to be either fast or *very fast*. (But like so many other bands I didn't quite "get" the first time around—Operation Ivy are another example—Neurosis would later become one of my all-time favorite bands.) The slampit during the other bands was, for lack of a better term, "fun." Most everyone was going in a clockwise circle knocking each other down and picking each other up, while the other jokers were going backwards or doing somersaults and cartwheels or playing chicken with people on their shoulders, and folks were obliged to sing along even if they didn't know the words. But during Neurosis the mood suddenly grew dark and depressing. It was no longer fun, but instead seemed like, I dunno, war. In hindsight their inclusion into the show made for a perfectly well-rounded experience. Punk rock, like life, wasn't all fun and horsing around—it was also mean and unsafe. Of course I was too young and dumb to realize it at the time, but deep down, I think I still somehow understood that.

In the end I left Gilman eager to return as quickly as possible. Big rock shows lasted all night and only showcased one-to-three bands, which were always totally unapproachable. But here was a place I could see five bands in one night, talk to each of them, and have enough money left over to buy all their records. Plus, unlike a rock show, there was something proactive about the event, something participatory. I wasn't going there to share a doobie in the parking lot and tune out. I was going there to tune in. And, in some form or another, I have been trying to stay tuned in ever since, so I think that right there says how influential the experience was.

I should also mention how that night I also brought home "that smell" which I've also carried with me ever since...

CH CH CH CH CHANGES

Rebecca Miller

The Situationists International formed in Paris, July 1957; their founding paper opened with the words:
First of all we think the world must be changed

In 1986 I was fifteen living with my parents in Redwood City, CA, a suburb thirty miles south of San Francisco. What was happening then is more complex than my fifteen-year-old's intentions at the time. I was not aware of my involvement in sophisticated and seminal creative gatherings. Punk, as with any culture, takes time and distance to understand its codes and ethics.

The main signifier that banded our high school punk community was some shaving of the head, usually the back or the sides, and some longer hair in the front—either sticking straight up or swinging sideways concealing one eye. We didn't have the one-stop punk rock shops that thrive today. Our get-ups were homemade and scavenged at the thrift store. The outfits for girls (which was basically the same for boys) were more uniform-like than fashion oriented, consisting of Mary Janes or china flat slippers, black or white t-shirts, striped leggings, long skirts, black eyeliner, and dangly gypsy earrings, bangle and black gummy bracelets. I would steal white v-neck t-shirts and zipper-front Dickies work shirts from my stepfather, Warren. My sister Sheila was five years older than me, going to hairdressing school, and listening to Bauhaus, Joy Division, and Tones on Tale. She was a glamour Goth. Her trip was more aesthetic than political—though I have often thought aesthetic representation is silent protest.

My boyfriend at the time introduced me to punk music. We had art class together and he asked me to draw him a spaceship. We were tight from that moment on. (Actually Jenny Martinez was the first punk I knew; we shaved our heads and ran away to 6th St. in S.F. in the sixth grade to go find my sister who was living in a hotel there.) He was a straight edge skater.

The first silkscreens I recall were in his record collection. Later, when I had to go to continuation high school, I would reproduce Samhain and Danzig album covers with an overhead projector and turn them into posters for him as tokens of love. I received art credits for this.

There was a punk that worked at Pony Express Pizza on Broadway (the main street in downtown Redwood City) and organized shows. As I recall, my first show was MDC, also known as Millions of Dead Cops, at the Pony. I e-mailed Dave Dictor, the singer of MDC, in Portland to confirm this happening and he wrote back and said he does remember this show: "Yes, I remember it… I don't remember much…it was an odd little show…hope we rocked you." MDC was living in San Francisco and had just released the *Smoke Signals* LP on Radical Records. I recall that Shawn Whitfield's band, Discontent, played with them. They screamed a lot. My Friend Greg Smith, who has been working for *Thrasher* forever, confirms this memory for me. He said: "Discontent at Pony Express, I remember the lady that worked there freaked out and was chasing people with a flashlight, it was pretty epic…"

My memories of this show are about as lucid as those of Dave Dictor. Perhaps it was clouded by the Robitussin, our beverage of choice. (This was a trick we learned by reading the *Basketball Diaries*.) I do remember how the night air in the suburbs felt, and remember enjoying the freedom of being out, hanging out with boys. It smells differently—like trees—and you can see the stars shine brightly just thirty miles outside of the city.

Inside the Pony, after shuffling a lot of equipment around, with man-boy punks bending over their instruments being very serious, the moment arrived. They pounded on the equipment and screamed a fast release of carnal energy accompanied by a primitive, backbone beat. The sound was more experiential and more difficult to understand than the romantic and digital goth pop I was exposed to. The songs/constructions were quick, sparse, loud accumulations and proliferations of unorthodox sounds that were not trained by formal standards. I can clearly see Shawn Whitfield's face in my mind: round, red, contorted, and screaming into the microphone. They were making this shit up. (I could not help but think about Shawn's tales of working in the hospital where he collected the fat after people had liposuctions, and the fact that he kept a fake boob implant in his bedroom—I knew this because my best friend dated him.) It was a conceptual performance, though no one knew about Dada yet. We reveled in our ability to explore and discover the awful truths of the world through music and performance. Anti-aesthetics emerged within us, defining what punk was by identifying what punk was not.

This event was secretive. We couldn't tell our parents what we were doing, but somehow we pulled it off. Going to the punk shows together with my friends created a bond that we didn't find at school or at home. It was a cabaret; everything was minimalist and detached from popular media culture as we knew it.

FINDING MY FAMILY: MY FIRST SHOW

Sto Cinders

We got on the train right after school that day. My junior high school was conveniently located right by a metro station, which was our salvation from suburban Virginia: a two dollar ticket to the freedom and debauchery that could be found in Washington, DC. Not to mention an all too tempting way to skip class, drop acid, and walk around the mall scaring tourists and scamming free hot dogs.

Chinatown was one of our favorite haunts. We would peruse the vast selection of ninja stars, nunchucks, butterfly knives, and tear gas at the kung fu shops. Once we were sufficiently stocked up, we'd head over to a run down restaurant, called Chopstix, to drink Mai Tai cocktails and feast on pu pu platters. I was a short, fresh-faced fourteen-year-old Asian boy, probably looked around eleven, and the oldest of our gang was barely sixteen. The people that ran the joint obviously did not give a FUCK! They would seat us in the way back at this big round table where we could stay hidden from other customers and they would just keep bringing on the drinks until we could hardly stand.

For a group of young punks, this place was heaven on earth. We were such regulars that we even had an on-going tab. Once adequately sauced, we would walk around playing with our new weapons like a small terrorist gang; a nasty combination of teen angst, alcohol, and abandon that would usually lead to minor injuries, caused by improper and inebriated use of our dangerous toys.

On this particular day, we started celebrating early because we were going to see the mighty Sick Of It All at the infamous 9:30 Club, home to legendary shows of punk yore, with the likes of Minor Threat and Bad Brains! Growing up in the DC area, I had heard mythic stories about Fugazi and Minor Threat by the time I was ten. I scored copies of *Margin Walker* and *Out of Step* by the time I was thirteen, and by then, the floodgates were open. I was regularly reading *MRR* and *Flipside,* and hanging out with some older kids that had actually been to shows before.

At this point I had only been to see Metallica at the Capital Centre on their "And Justice For All…" tour when I was nine…with my Dad. Do you know embarrassing it is to be seen headbanging next to your Dad? Needless to say, I was ecstatic to be going to a real "show" with my friends at a legendary punk club.

We made our way to the back of Chopstix for some egg rolls and several rounds of cocktails. I had been saving my lunch money the past two weeks and was now spending it wisely on pre-show alcohol consumption. The 9:30 Club was named so because of its location: 930 F Street, and we were literally right around the corner, waiting in anticipation.

After wearing out our welcome at the restaurant (a combination of Ben puking on the table, and Marty lighting matches and throwing them at everyone probably did it), we decided to go for a walk and attempt to buy beer somewhere. As we walked along H Street, Ben had the brilliant idea to try out his tear gas at no one in particular, but as he shot some out in front of us, a big gust of wind threw it right back into our faces. Aaarggh! We got on all fours right there in the middle of Chinatown's main strip, crying like little babies, blinded for what seemed like hours.

The pain wore off after about ten minutes, and with puffy eyes and red faces, we managed to buy 40s of Old English 800 and crawl up a concrete wall on F Street to hide amongst the trees and drink in peace. It was a great drinking spot; you could see people down below on the sidewalk, but they couldn't see you. I remember thinking, "This is the life." As day turned to night, the atmosphere of the street had also changed dramatically: from suit and tie guys and gals to homeless dudes spare-changing and punk kids milling about. The time had finally come: "Let's go to the show!!"

I sprang up fast and realized that I had downed an exorbitant amount of alcohol, undoubtedly more than I ever had in my short life. I felt funny and lightheaded, a white hot pain shot through my stomach and then it happened: a projectile waterfall of fried eggroll bits and malt liquor spewed down the wall and onto the sidewalk, hitting the homeless guy below us. "WHAARAGGH!" he yelled unintelligibly up at the trees where we hid. He stormed off, everyone laughing at him and then at me: doubled over, dry-heaving, wiping my mouth with my sleeve, ugh.

Alas I got it all out and actually started to feel better, just the right amount of drunken buzz and post-puke clarity, ready for my first punk show! We made our way through 9:30's ominous doors, which I had previously seen photographed in the book *Banned in DC*, our harDCore picture bible which was studied over and over for its insightful anecdotes and punk fashion tips. I'll never forget the smell of that dingy hallway—part cavernous must, part body odor and sweat—the pheromones reeling me inside.

Our older friend Donovan was already there, wearing a 7-11 convenience store uniform he had gotten out of their dumpster, grinning and greeting us with hugs. I was wearing my much-coveted Samhain shirt (the one with their faces all bloody), which he always tried to haggle off of me every time I had it on.

The first band was already midway through their set. They were called Sheer Terror and they were real LOUD. Arena shows were of course much louder, but being in such close proximity to the stage and the speakers, I could feel the sound hit me hard. The band's singer, Paul Bearer, was angry, tattooed, fat, and had a gravely singing style. They were really good; they covered the Cure's "Boys Don't Cry" in a real mocking way, and I practiced my dance moves along the outer edges of the pit.

Yes, the PIT—at the 9:30! It was both weirdly exciting and scary to see people slamming into each other, jumping off the stage, fists raised, heads bouncing up and down. It felt easy to get lost in the wave of mass momentum, and I almost got pulled into the circle, but chickened out and made my way to the back. I surveyed the atmosphere: crusty punks, skinheads, hardcore dudes, and a couple of Goth kids looking bored by the bar. Not many girls! Where were the ladies?

I really felt at home though; a safe place for freaks like me and my friends, a place where people looked stranger than me... Imagine that! I explored while the others danced, looking at all the faces in the crowd, bravely descending into the basement lit with black light. My teeth looked funny and florescent in the mirror and my clothes looked really dirty and dusty. There were old flyers for shows plastered on the walls, floors, and tables—Misfits, Necros, Black Market Baby, GI—some I knew and some I tried to remember for later investigation.

I sat alone at a table and tried to take in the moment of my first show, tracing the words "All Ages" with my finger from the flyer that was glued to the table. I felt part of something for the first time. It was my secret and no one at school would ever be this cool. My friends found me and dragged me upstairs; Sick Of It All was about to hit the stage!

They pulled me to the very front, brushing up against sweaty skin and hair, weaving through bodies, losing air, and feeling out of breath. Then they came out, these burly looking New York guys, and with the first note of "It's Clobberin' Time!" my friend Donovan ran across the stage and flipped right over us into the sea of bodies. Time seemed to stand still as I was pushed into the pit and then shoved around, my dance moves kinda falling apart as I began to just try and protect myself from fists and bodies.

I was getting kicked pretty hard from behind and when I turned around to confront the culprit, I found a couple of skinhead girls smiling and taunting me. What was I gonna do about it? Nothing. I was alone and they had big boyfriends. I had heard all about those kind of girls, picking up guys with brand new Doc Martens, and then bringing them into the alley behind the 9:30 for their boyfriends to beat up and steal their boots. Brutal. I just moved to the side and watched them kick other folks for a while, and then pulled myself up on top of one of the PA speakers.

It was a great view up there; the chaos was fun to watch from a safe distance, and I could actually pay attention to the band. As they were about to go into a cover of Minor Threat's "Betray," I was told to get down from my perch by one of the club's bouncers. As the song began, the crowd erupted into a frenzy and with the only option of getting down that I had, I dove on top of people's heads as they cheered me on, passing me around and across the entire crowd to the other side of the club. My first stage-dive! I was thrilled and felt totally complete.

I headed for the exit, completely soaked with sweat and high from crowd surfing. I stumbled outside and pulled out a very bent Marlboro Red from my mangled pack and sat against the wall. The sidewalk was full of activity: kids talking, passing out flyers for other shows, laughing, smiling, and also nearly fist-fighting. It was all so exciting and I knew that this is where I truly belonged—not on a sports team or in the math league or hanging out with the preps from school at their lame parties.

I was a punk and THIS was my family.

AT SEVENTEEN I LEARNED THE TRUTH

Michael Azerrad

In April of '78 some street toughs knifed Dead Boys drummer Johnny Blitz on the mean streets of the East Village and left him for dead. The Dead Boys' medical benefits plan was apparently not up to snuff, so the rest of the band did a series of benefit shows for Blitz, who was still in the hospital weeks after the incident. Just about every band who regularly played CBGB at the time joined in, the original punk community uniting to help one of its own—that was very cool. I caught one of those shows. It was my first time to CBGB, and it was the night before my 17th birthday.

My friends and I had discovered punk rock when one of us came back from a trip to England with an armload of punk singles, posters and badges by bands like the Clash, the Damned, the Sex Pistols and the Stranglers. It blew our minds and it truly changed my life. So now we were punks. In safe suburban Westchester. When we heard the Dead Boys were playing at CBGB, we had to go.

We had no idea how late things ran in the big city so we showed up early, I guess also just to get our money's worth. We were clearly under age, but the guy at the door let us in, no problem; downtown New York was kind of lawless then—like the Wild West, but smellier. These days even the dinkiest clubs run your driver's license through a machine that reveals whether you're a wanted criminal. At CBGB, though, beers were $4, which was totally astronomical in 1978. Maybe they were gouging us because we were kids, I don't know. But it meant that we didn't drink more than one beer the whole night.

We saw Helen Wheels, who we didn't think was punk at all—it just seemed like all the hard rock we'd heard already. Then Shrapnel came on and they were more punk; word was Norman Mailer was a fan, but for us their claim to fame was that they covered the *Underdog* theme. Then this really scary-looking band came out sporting pale green face paint, black uniforms and armbands with quasi-Nazi insignia. Whoah, creepsville. Then it was the Corpse Grinders, Arthur "Killer" Kane's new band, who were pretty good but never did amount to anything.

We were leaning against the north wall of the club, our heels up on beer bottles so we could see over the crowd better. I was standing next to my friend Charlie. (Along with a few other buddies, we had a punk band called the Monads. The chorus to our theme song: "Well, I'm a Monad/ And you're all gonads." We shoulda been huge.) Above our heads, stapled to the wall right over the already dense agglomeration of band flyers encrusting every vertical surface of the place, were empty album covers of *Talking Heads '77*. Funny thing was, they all had dozens of stab marks in them, like they'd been attacked by, you know, a psycho killer. I pulled one down and held onto it all night. I still have it. Anyway, early in the evening one of us spotted Legs McNeil in the crowd. Legs had co-founded *Punk* magazine, which made him a major celebrity in our eyes. And I suppose it still does. Every time Legs walked through the club I would point him out to Charlie, then holler, "LEGS!" and quickly turn away. Legs would turn around to see who was calling, see Charlie looking right at him, and stare daggers at him. Eventually, I thought Legs was going to kill Charlie so I stopped.

At last the Dead Boys came on, and they *rocked*. (Then again, any band with Jerry Nolan on drums rocked.) Stiv was like a rat, pointy-faced and lithe, stalking the stage in his heart-shaped sunglasses and snazzy jacket, too cool, and the rest of the band was totally bad-ass, the very picture of a punk rock band. Guitarist Cheetah Chrome, sporting an undersized Cub Scout shirt, was so wasted he had to play part of the set sitting in a chair. They played all the hits: "I Need Lunch," "All This and More," "Ain't Nothing to Do."

In the middle of the set, John Belushi, from an obscure, late-night sketch comedy show on NBC, came up and played drums on "Sonic Reducer." And he was pretty good! Later on, legendary drag queen Divine, along with a bevy of bumping, grinding, semi-naked women, came up and danced with Stiv, completely dwarfing him, which was hilarious. I don't think I'd ever seen a transvestite before.

During the encores, Stiv hauled his hot girlfriend onto the stage. I don't know who she was—maybe Bebe Buell? They kind of wrestled each other to the floor, whereupon Stiv began dry-humping her with utterly unself-conscious abandon. I'd never seen anything like that before either. It was a few minutes after midnight. I'd just turned 17!

FUCK 4-H, BUT THANK GOD FOR THE FAIRGROUNDS

Shannon Stewart

Nothing really stands out for people when you say you are from Eastern Washington. People might jump to associate it with Seattle, the rise of coffee, flannel, and of course, the bands that comprise the soundtrack to the movie *Singles*.

For better or for worse, I grew up in an indie scene about 220 miles away from the grunge Mecca, just as its novelty was fading with the hairlines and jean washes of the Sub Pop legends.

An eyebrow might rise if you say the word "Hanford," indicating faint recognition of the nuclear wasteland that my parents relocated us to Texas from. Close proximity to Hanford, explains the "nuke 'em till they glow!" slogans on team jerseys and sweatshirts for my alma matter, Richland High School, home of the Bombers.

No, I'm not kidding. That was really the slogan.

My discontent in this surreal world started in the form of an addiction to black comedy, and *Yo! MTV Raps* followed by *Headbanger's Ball*. In all honesty, the soundtrack for *Pump Up The Volume*, led me to the Descendents, the Pixies, Sonic Youth, Bad Brains and MC5. Post-jr. high, I found myself on a determined quest to find my comrades who saw through the façade of our perfectly manufactured whitebread lives.

It turns out, I did eventually find them at the Tri-City Hoedown, a squaredance shack that alternative kids flocked to on the weekends to see bands such as Treepeople, Engine Kid, Schedule, Small, Crown, One Eye Open, Ladybird Union, and the occasional grunge stop through by Black Happy, Lucky Me, Screaming Trees, Sweaty Nipples, The Gits (a few nights before Mia was murdered), Tkchung!, and probably some more notable acts that I was too young to recognize the names of.

Being in this shadow of grunge, and a long way from punk's incarnate in pop form, my initiation into punk wasn't really punk at all. I imagine it was exactly the same as a lot of kids from all over the country that were like me. Bailing out of sports and stuffing the evidence of MC Hammer concerts in the closet until I went to see Fugazi at the local Fairgrounds. It wasn't an intimate show in a moldy basement where I could taste the sweat of fellow showgoers accumulating on my skin, while my eardrums were berated with three chords blaring out of a blown PA. It was a live-stock warehouse where hundreds of kids hungry for subversion, lined up and paid their $5 to see local favorites open for the beacons of hope for misunderstood youth everywhere: Guy, Ian, Joe, and Brendan.

You can read *Our Band Could Be Your Life* to get an idea of where I could go with this. At that show, for the first time, I saw performers that not only played good music, but were smart, espoused things about equality, took care of the crowd, had confidence without being narcissists. I was a lifetime fan forever more.

But truth be told, I went to that Fugazi show to see Small, the band that had less than two seconds of MTV fame for singing "Legalize It (Marijuana)," which was more notoriety than any other Tri-City band had had. While kids all over their world stopped washing their hair and started ripping their clothes, in the Tri-Cities, we were beyond sick of grunge—we were allergic. The band boys (and the bands were almost exclusively boys of course) were tapering their uniform pants, wearing tight button up shirts and slicking their hair back in a style somewhere in between rockabilly and Crispin Glover circa his nerdy version in *Back to the Future*.

And then there was the Diet Pepsi.

Oh the Diet Pepsi.

These boys all carried around two liter bottles of Diet Pepsi wherever they went. Wallet chains dangling out of their Dickies as accessory along with a two liter bottle in hand. Completely dreamy.

I thought the rhythms were mathy, but I'm not sure I knew what mathy was. Songs were short epics, usually referencing a party spot somewhere out in the sage bush. They were local kids singing about the stuff that mattered the most to all of us who were forced to grow up there.

> *Where I stand*
> *I stood a younger man*
> *And now I know*
> *These trees they feel like home*

And since the younger days
They should have stayed the same
They won't be back
To bring us back again

...Gather my friends
Bring us back again
                —"Out at the Delta" by Small

In reality, this scene's greatest claim to fame was Built to Spill's precursor band: Treepeople. Nonetheless, I had, and still have, an intense amount of pride and was made into a music scenester that will always have a focus on the über local.

I can't remember much else about that first show, potentially because I didn't really understand the straight edge thing (nor did the promoter who booked Fugazi with Small). But what's more likely is that I was focused on hanging out with my random assortment of misfit pals in what finally felt like a community where I fit in. At the fairgrounds, at the Hoedown, out at the Delta, we could accept that "Feeling screwed up at a screwed up time in a screwed up place does not necessarily make you screwed up."—Mark Hunter (aka Christian Slater in *Pump up the Volume*)

LITTLE BOY BLUE AND THE MAN IN THE MOON

Scott Bourne

Trying to recall, now, all of the bands my young mind was exposed to, conjures up a perplexity of punk rock memories. Growing up on a small family farm in the Carolinas, my immediate environment was anything but punk rock. My mind is haunted, in the most peaceful way, by visions of my father (quickly drunk from a single glass of wine) grabbing my mother from the dining room table, and leading her into a romantic dance to the music of Kenny Rogers' "Lady"… At this time in my young life, I had no idea just how punk Kenny Rogers—or my father—was.

The small town I grew up in was neatly located on the outskirts of both Chapel Hill and Raleigh. With the speed of ignorance and youth, one could make it to Chapel Hill in about twenty minutes and on to Raleigh in less than half an hour. I was sixteen or seventeen and had just gotten my operator's. Growing up in a small town as I did, the procurement of a driver's license was like having a passport to the world. All of

a sudden, everything was within reach. Chapel Hill was still a small college town, but the music scene had just begun to boom. The local club
that booked all the bands was called the Cat's Cradle. That stage would
host the first punk and alternative bands I was exposed to. It is strange
to think back on that club now, on its name, and how it has seemed
to follow me. Years later, while returning to visit my family, I would find
myself in a Carolina jail cell where I read a copy of Vonnegut's novel
Cat's Cradle—probably five times—before making bail. My father would
die that very morning as I stepped out into the sun. Years down the
road, I would hear Harry Chapin's song "Cat's in the Cradle" and with a
haunted sense of sorrow, would realize it had become the soundtrack of
my life. I was living on the road, traveling the world, and had lost almost
all sense of home or family. Looking back now, it only seems fitting that
these things should have affected my life in such an incredible way, and
that my stomping ground as a young punk rocker was none other than
the Cat's Cradle; a sort of foreshadowing for the events of my life.

The small town where I lived was just out of reach of the college
radio station in Chapel Hill, which was 88.5 or 88.7, depending on what
car you were in. In the mornings, on the way to school, the car would
pass close enough to the station to pick up transmission. An announcer
called out shows and dates. Always, my ears were tuned. It was there at
the Cat's Cradle that I first saw bands like Polvo, Archers of Loaf, Brick
Bat, Geezer Lake, and Superchunk. The music scene was alive and very
creative. For the first time, North Carolina was getting attention for the
bands it was producing. In the span of just a few months, my friends and
I had all turned sixteen. One of us could always get a car off our parents,
or score a ride from an older brother, and for a while, not a weekend
went by that we weren't at a show. Before long, we were off to neigh-
boring cities like Raleigh, Durham, Wilmington, Winston, and Charlotte,
sometimes venturing as far as Richmond, being careful to not let our
parents know just how far we had gone.

Now that I am approaching thirty, it is strange for me to go back in
my mind over all the bands I have seen, listened to, and loved in the last
fifteen years of the punk rock experience. The list of bands I have seen
live is pretty incredible and spans from They Might be Giants to Dylan,
from Rollins to Springsteen. I have seen the Circle Jerks, Jawbreaker, Mo-
torhead, and KISS!, Will Oldham, Samiam, Crooked Fingers, Ted Nugent,
Sting, Firehose, Ani Difranco, Shelter, Bad Religion, Sonic Youth, and the

US Bombs. I've seen so many bands I can't even recall them all... But if I were to speak of the first punk band I ever saw, it would most definitely be Fugazi.

I believe it was their first tour, or at least the first time they played anywhere near my town. I had first heard about the band from my friend, Andrew Alvey. He made me a tape of their first album, which I had played so much that my friends had already begun to hate it. You couldn't get in a car with me without being subjected to Fugazi. Being that I was the only one with my own car, my friends were at my mercy. News that the band was going to play at the Cat's Cradle had reached me by phone. A friend who lived nearly three hours away had found out about it, and was already putting out the word. Immediately, I made a trip to School Kids Records (which was the cool record store in Chapel Hill at the time...maybe still is) and purchased a ticket—a five dollar ticket, quite possibly the best-spent five bucks of my entire youth. The day of the show was full of excitement and energy. My buddies and I had all cut school and spent the day in Chapel Hill skating the university. A few hours before the show, we stopped by School Kids to check out some records. From outside the record store, my friend Jon Dell spied Ian and Guy flipping through some records. Before I knew it, Jon yelled out a line from one of their songs and quickly skated off. I stood there, stupidly looking in at Ian. Just seeing them inside the record store reassured me that they were real people just like you or me.

That night, as they took the stage, I pushed my way up to the front of the crowd. At the time, I had long hair and wore it pulled back in a pony-tail. I remember being the only one in the crowd with long hair. Even the girls had short or shaved heads. As soon as the band started to play, everyone began to pulsate to the music and chant the lyrics. It was the first time I had ever seen a band have this effect on a crowd. To this day, I can still remember just how everything happened the day leading up to and after the show. When I left the show that night, I could not get the songs and sensations out of my head. Some of them are still with me to this day. The next day, I showed up at Tom Summey's—he'd been with us at the show. He shaved my head right then and there, and all of a sudden, I was a punk rocker.

Looking back on it now, it all seems a bit comical to me, but it was a time of experiment and change, and that is exactly what it means to me to be "punk rock." It means that, through a musical experience, something happens to you. It means that a feeling is invoked and one cannot help but act upon it. I had seen many bands before Fugazi, but I just didn't know something could happen. Seeing that band, on that night, altered my vision of the world around me. It was that experience that permitted me to see how punk Kenny Rogers *actually* was. The way he could inspire my father to grab the woman he loved and dance through the house with her in front of his two children, causing the entire house to be filled with love, was definitely punk.

The last time I saw Fugazi was exactly ten years to the day from that first show. It was a free concert in Dolores Park, SF, and was the day before I would take my first journey to Europe…and again they had set a brilliant scene for change.

—Train ride from Toulouse to Paris. February 17, 2003

ROCKED HOTEL

Trivikrama das

My concert experiences were pretty limited up until my first hard-core show on New Year's Eve, 1983 (1984?). I had seen Laurie Anderson, Devo, and Public Image Limited, all of which blew my mind, but my first hardcore show transformed me in a different way. My sister Jacqui, who passed away in 1987, took me to the show, which took place on Jane Street in the west village, at a club called Rock Hotel. My sister had been in and out of boarding schools and reform institutions, where she had connected with a bunch of friends involved in the hardcore scene. She herself was more of a psychedelic, Grateful Dead fan and a barefoot traveler, but being very much an outsider of mainstream society, she was akin to the hardcore punkers who befriended her as she moved along the outskirts of "the norm." The bands playing were Circle Jerks, Murphy's Law, and Kraut.

As we walked down Jane Street to the show, a few people recognized my sister and said hi to her. A guy named Matt Ross, wearing a leather jacket and sporting a devil lock, asked Jacqui how a mutual friend named Allison Stein was doing. She was locked up in the school my sister had run away from and had lent my sister an amazing collection of hardcore records that I had been listening to: Blitz, the Dead Kennedys, The Misfits, a world of music which I was quickly absorbing and which I felt a great affinity with.

A tall young man with buzzed blond hair and a leather vest (Joe Bruno) stood by the door as we entered the Rock Hotel. It was dark inside, and a world of leather jacketed, spiky-headed boys and girls lined the walls upstairs and downstairs. Girls in plaid skirts with fishnet stockings, smelling of aqua-net, and boys with shaved heads, no shirts, and tattoos seemed poised to explode as they waited for the first band to start. "We're Murphy's Law," the singer yelped.

The place went crazy; people were climbing on top of each other, singing along, combat boots diving into the mob. I was astounded to witness this nighttime world of music and people who were outsiders, united to rock. The music was really loud, gritty, and powerful. The guitar player (Uncle Al) seemed older than the rest, and played a red Gibson SG through a Marshall stack. The sound was pure and fully rocked.

I loved it. I was not familiar with much of the band's music, maybe a few songs from listening to the radio shows *Hellhole*, and *Rude Awakening*, but did know "Wild thing" and "Stepping Stone," which they played. The relationship of the crowd and the band struck me. The audience merged with the music. The ensuing chaos of bodies flying to the beat of the hyper-speed songs seemed an amazing marriage.

When they finished, I waited in awe, looking around in the dark at all the assembled characters, who had such interesting individualized styles and physical traits: a man older than the rest, with spiky blonde hair and a patch over his eye; a young man, named Dave, with a leather jacket, freshly shaven head, and a prominent stutter; and a girl with thick black eyeliner, white bleached hair, a sleeveless and ripped white t-shirt, and black leather pants burned themselves into my memory forever.

After what seemed like a long time in the dark, the lights came on and Kraut hit the stage. Their songs had more bounce in them and the crowd responded by pogo-ing or jumping up and down. The lights were on and I fixated on the sounds coming from the guitar player's Les Paul, adorned with an iron cross sticker and coil cord. This band seemed to be more serious and in control than Murphy's Law. The danger, darkness, and chaos seemed to lift as they played, as they exhibited a more orderly, springy, punk sound.

My sister and I had to leave after Kraut played, missing the headlining band, the Circle Jerks. I was disappointed to leave the Rock Hotel, but I was forever changed. From that day forward I attended every hardcore show I possibly could, taking risks by sneaking out of my house and sneaking in to see groups like Agnostic Front, Cro-mags, Reagan Youth, and the Psychos. My "first time" catapulted me into a world of underground music that would inform my choices for a long time to come.

MOSQUITOES AND WHISKEY

Chris Walter

Living away from home alleviated a lot of tension. I hated my parents less. Once in a while, I would drop by to wash some clothes and have a real Sunday supper. At least we could talk to each other for short periods of time without screaming.

I went to Windsor Park on my day off to do some laundry and raid the refrigerator. I had managed to negotiate a temporary ceasefire with my brother, Jim. He was, after all, a fellow Sick Crew member. He had some money and wanted to get some new albums, so we took a bus downtown and walked into the closest record store. Row upon row of horrible albums covered the walls—Boston, Foreigner, Toto, Journey, Styx—it was enough to make a deaf man puke. We didn't know what we wanted, but we knew what we *didn't* want. Being older and supposedly more hip, I felt it was my duty to know which albums to buy. The truth was I didn't have a clue. Neither did Jim. We wandered around the store staring dumbly at all the gaudy '70s dinosaur rock. We both felt pressure to buy a new album. There had to be something good somewhere.

In desperation, we moved to the front of the store to scan the new releases. Those records looked really bad too, but one name was familiar: the Ramones—and they had a new album.

Jim picked it up first. "This looks cool. But who are the Ramones?" he said, examining the cover.

"These guys are good," I said. "Let's get this."

Jim paid for the record and we took it back to the suburbs. We had no idea of the impact this record would make on our lives. Jim slapped the new album onto his jury-rigged stereo and turned it up loud enough to give the cat a heart attack. There were no guitar solos, no drum solos—no solos of any kind. Just blistering two-minute blasts of punk rock brilliance.

We loved it.

Dad stuck his head inside the door of Jim's room and screamed over the music. "Turn that gawdawful racket down!" he bellowed. No punk rocker, he.

Jim quickly did as requested. When Dad went back downstairs, Jim turned it up again, but not quite as loud as it had been. I almost wrecked the album for Jim by singing along to it. The best thing about the Ramones was that you didn't have to be a rocket scientist to appreciate what they had to offer. I later discovered that they were harder to imitate than one would think. The Ramones only made it look easy.

We went looking for other punk albums. The Sex Pistols, after many delays, had finally released their first album. We quickly purchased it and left the store. As we walked down Portage Avenue to the bus stop, a poster in a window caught Jim's eye. "Hey, check this out," he said, pointing.

The crude poster made from cutout magazines advertised five bands for a dollar. We had never heard of any of the bands, but what did it matter? The show was scheduled to be held at the University of Manitoba the following Friday.

"Let's go," we said.

Other than liquor, drugs, and girls, music was becoming increasingly important. When the stereo was cranked up really high, all other problems faded into insignificance. When the Ramones sang "I Don't Care," they summed it up for me perfectly. I felt that if I weren't able to channel off some teenage angst I would end up in very serious trouble. Punk rock had arrived just in time.

My outward appearance hadn't changed as a result of punk. I still had long hair and bell-bottom pants. I'd seen the occasional weirdo downtown with spiky hair, black peg leg jeans, and combat boots, but punk clothing had not caught on at all. You couldn't buy punk gear anywhere. If you wanted to dress punk, you had to make your own clothes. Not only that, but it took guts to look different. People felt threatened by anything they weren't familiar with, and in Winnipeg, this translated to *look out!* Those first few brave souls who had the guts to dye their hair, wear ripped clothing, or dog collars were beaten often and badly.

The night of the show arrived. Jim and I nervously took the long bus ride out to the university campus. It was very cold and we didn't know our way around. We were lost.

"Brrr," Jim shivered. "Where is this fuckin' place?"

An old car slid to a stop, and four strange looking people disembarked. Safety pins and chains dripped from ripped clothing, and their spiky hair appeared to have been slathered with dayglo paint. They were very drunk and I didn't blame them. You would need a lot of liquid courage to go outside dressed like that.

"Let's follow these guys," I wisely suggested.

Sure enough, the bizarre group led us directly to the hall where they were holding the show. Jim and I paid our dollar to a little guy with a skinny tie and went inside. Onstage, a band was playing. The singer was very tall and thin. He hunched over the microphone as if it was a toy. The music they played bore little resemblance to the Ramones. It was fast, but way out of kilter and out of tune. I couldn't hear any of the words because the guitars were much louder than the vocals and completely drowned him out. What the band may have lacked in talent they made up for in enthusiasm. They bounced around and fell down, but kept playing. It looked like fun. My brother found a couple of paper cups and poured us a drink from the mickey he had smuggled into the show. Other people were openly drinking from bottles and appeared to be very drunk. When the band stopped playing, they were rewarded with jeers and volleys of spit.

"FUCK YOU!" said the singer spewing a mouthful of beer back at his antagonists.

I didn't know what the hell was going on. I had never seen anything like this before. The next band came on. They were drunker than the last band and even louder. A few people hopped up and down in front of the stage. I realized they must be pogoing. I had read about this somewhere. It looked silly, but oddly appealing. I watched the band struggle along and a thought came to me: *anyone can do this.*

Then a fight broke out between what looked like a couple of drunken frat boys. There were no bouncers, so the fight carried on until both combatants were bleeding and exhausted. The band finished their set and left the stage to a chorus of boos and some random clapping. The next day I couldn't remember what they sounded like. It was all glorious noise.

Five bands for a dollar? I could hardly wait for the next show.

MY TEN SPEED ON THE INTERSTATE

Rusty Mahakian

When I was eleven or twelve, my older sister dated a dirty seaman.
He fled Orange County for the Navy, and he was now stuck in the East
Bay. He would come over to our house, the one with shag carpets—one
on a long list of dirty rental properties each of my parents separately
rotated through. He brought over a copy of *Another State of Mind* and
I scrawled "Mommy's Little Monster" on my junior high book bag. My
sister started siphoning down tapes from twenty-five-year-old art punks
she worked with at a salad bar. She was big into goth, and in this era, so
ripe with soc's and assholes, having an earring or army boots put you on
a social blacklist that included most everyone in the margins. I lived five
miles from Berkeley, but I could have been on the North Pole. When my
sister left, my access to the outside world did as well. The Doors and
Mexican weed were a lot easier to get your hands on, and no matter

how spot-on retarded Jim Morrison's writing was, at its very least, it was expression at a time when I needed it.

In late 1991, a firestorm engulfed the East Bay, and my Boy Scout troop mobilized to fight the fire. I put out a bunch of small fires that day and I met this guy Hamilton who went to St. Mary's College. We walked home together; he lived in the same retirement community my mom bought a condo in. He seemed equally miserable, being the only black guy in a sea of old white people, as he rented a room from a 140-year-old lady down the street. Hamilton was an insane record collector. His room consisted of a bed, a Mac, and ten crates of records—and he had everything. I saw the Jawbreaker cat, and I wanted a tape. The album spoke to me, and from their inception, Jawbreaker insisted on rocking. They captured the feeling my sister's friends gave me: of inclusion, and that knowing about things was cool, and that cops sucked. I knew little of their world, but I wanted to know more.

I saw a flyer for a show where Jawbreaker would open up for Mr. T Experience and Samiam on a Sunday night. The show was early enough to check out, so my pal Wolf and I decided to make the trip. We showed up 3 hours early.

Wolf was wearing an irony-free, pink polo shirt, and I was wearing something I attribute to the Doors. The stage was a foot tall and there were about twenty of us. The band put everything together and used the microphones to talk about riding BART to the show. I remember thinking that these three guys about to play music were cooler than us—but not that much cooler. It wasn't about being anything but yourself; it was hard to front when you sing about "a fine day" or about "wanting" someone.

I remember rocking out with a repressed "everyone is staring at me" overbite, and I remember bobbing. I started dreaming about Jawbreaker: they would come for coffee, attend my grandmother's funeral, and it was cool to have them around because falling off cliffs alone was just a shitty way to dream.

They were my first ten-speed on the interstate. They were wheels, and that show opened my world to the nooks and crannies of industrial neighborhoods, zines, and work pants (a much more comfortable fit). My network grew; I met more people, and I read more.

I loved many bands, but with each release, Jawbreaker became smarter; from the cover art to the music to the words, each album was ripe with emotion...And not the no-eye contact shield of ice, cages full of Modest Mice-front in the streets today. It was tangible art for art's sake, that had heart, but rocked, first and foremost. They became cool, and at my last college—the same college Blake tried to burn down in the late-80s—I heard they signed to Geffen. They were my first, and we had lost them. I typed a short letter about how hurt I was that they had signed. Within three days, I received a hand-written note from Blake. He said that I shouldn't take it as a slap in the face, this was a risk, and that things change. He talked about meeting Steve Ignorant in England, and ended the note by saying he was in a bar, drunk.

SKEENO HARDCORE GIG ENDS TOO LATE FOR FOURTEEN-YEAR-OLD ME

Pete Slovenly

My first punk rock gig was in Sparks, Nevada (on the border with Reno) at the Red Rose Dance hall, in 1988. The venue used to be a bowling alley—nowadays I think it's called the New Oasis. I was four-teen years old, and had waited for this with more excited anticipation than any other show I can remember. My favorite punk band, Circle Jerks, were coming to town to play a show with 7 Seconds, D*Vision, and Damaged. And I was on the guest list, because my best friend's big brother's bandmate was the guy who organized the show. As if that wasn't good enough, at 4 pm on the day of it, there was an in-store band appearance at my neighborhood record store, UR What You Play!

I put my Circle Jerks "VI" shirt on and pedaled my ass up the hill to the shop. I got there late, but caught the band as they were leaving.

Apparently no one had shown up to meet them. So I was the only one, and I had the chance to tell the guys how much I loved the band, and get a photo or two. I didn't ask for autographs because that was rock star bullshit. Keith Morris scolded me for having a bootleg t-shirt. I didn't know what bootleg meant at the time, and I coasted back down the hill towards the cul de sac a bit confused and afraid that I'd done something terribly wrong...

My best friend and I arrived early to the gig so we got to see all the sound checks and everything. We even hung out backstage with his big brother and the members of all the bands. I felt really lucky, and also really at home in a way. Which doesn't surprise me too much now—in the eighteen years that have passed since, practically everything I've been busy with is connected in some way or another with music...

I watched as a line formed outside the club. It stretched all the way around the corner. The gig was totally packed. People started warming up during the first band, Damaged. I don't remember liking them too much. But already during the second band, D*Vision, blood was shed. The circle pit was pretty violent—I thought people were fighting. It was especially confusing to me considering the high-pitched voice of the singer, and the one song I remember, which was about Oreo cookies. I stayed away, at first in the back but then sticking closer to the stage to see the bands...

7 Seconds were great, of course, and tons of kids were freaking the fuck out. (In case you don't know, 7 Seconds put Reno on the punk rock map by releasing a single on Alternative Tentacles, and recording some classic punk rock albums on their own label, Positive Force Records.) Skeeno hardcore was alive and well (though already dying by '88), and violent. I saw some kid leave early, because he had to, otherwise, he probably would have bled to death. I wasn't going anywhere though, not without seeing the Circle Jerks.

Of course, the Circle Jerks were fantastic. While they were playing someone told me that one of the guys from the band was from Reno, and worked at my neighborhood instrument shop, Bizarre Guitar. But we couldn't figure out if he was still in the band or just played on one of the older records. After the gig I went backstage to congratulate the band, and hung out with my friend and his big brother, until I realized that it was getting pretty late. I called my mom on the payphone to come pick me up.

I left through the backstage door and walked to the corner, where I told my mom I'd wait for her. Within minutes, a police car rolled up and the officer asked me what I was doing out so late. It was around midnight. Before I could answer, he blurted, "How old are you, son? Let me see some ID."

I showed him my high school identification card and he told me to get into the car.

Confused, I pleaded with the officer, "But I'm waiting for my mom, she's on her way to pick me up right now!"

"She can pick you up from the station."

Yeah, I was arrested for curfew the night of my first punk rock show. And my poor ma showed up minutes after Officer Friendly hauled me off to the police station. Remember, this happened long before cell phones, so my worried mom drove around looking for me for an hour before finally giving up and going home to call the police. When she got there, my stepdad had taken the message that I was waiting at the Sparks Police Department.

She came to pick me up, and on the way home swore that she'd never let me go to any more "rock concerts"... But of course I found a way to go to plenty more, and eighteen years later I still haven't seen enough.

HOW A PUNK'S MOTHER BECAME A BOUNCER!

Ann Kanaan

Far from being the typical eleven- to sixteen-year-old, I was forty-one when I attended my first punk concert—and then only to enable the show to take place! My son Ramsey and his three co-performers were putting on a gig for Women's Aid—a charity for which I was a volunteer. Barely an hour before they were due to begin, Ramsey phoned home from the center where they were setting up, and with deep disappoint-ment in his voice, said they were not allowed to play because they had no "bouncers"—stringent rules of the Community Hall, apparently. We lived in a small town in Scotland, called Stirling. In 1982, punks were a rare and intimidating breed, especially to my age-group and older. All that metal and black leather and wild hair arrangements were more than enough to guarantee we more conventional folk averted our gaze and crossed the road whenever we saw any of them, usually in "gangs," ap-proaching. On one memorable occasion, a startled neighbor, commenting on the logo painted on Ramsey's leather jacket, said, "You know, your son is a nice boy, but why does he want to *poison girls!?*"

Now, I had spent many months sighing and remonstrating at the incredible volume of noise that Political Asylum made whenever they practiced (far too often) in a room at the back of the house—generally to the order of, "Can't you make less racket? The neighbors will be complaining again." But this was different. This was my boy who was thwarted by officialdom, and he was upset. Within the hour, there were five bouncers including a couple of staunch male friends, two volunteers from Women's Aid, and myself at the premises. Oh, and Ramsey's wee brother, Ali, aged five, as there was no one I could leave him with at such short notice.

The men were real stalwarts. One was "on the door" and his role was to check for, and remove, any metal objects from the audience. The other was to be on duty in the men's toilets (I still have only a guess at what his job entailed). I was placed in the hall where the music and dancing was to take place—a hall that was much respected by the other users of the centre, such as the Bingo Club or the Seniors Lunch Group, as it had been newly restored. My job was to ensure that no cigarette ends were stubbed out on the shiny wooden floor—and therefore I was to prevent anyone from even lighting up. Maybe I should say that I am not very big—pretty damn small, in fact—and not particularly brave, and there were a lot of very tough looking young people in there, even when divested of much of their metal. And sure enough, as I looked around apprehensively, crossing all fingers that my bouncing skills would not be tested, a very large, very aggressive looking punk, looking straight at me, slowly and deliberately took out a cigarette and raised it to his lips. The gauntlet had been thrown and I knew I had to rise to the challenge. In the time that it took for me to reach him, all eyes were upon us.

"Excuse me," I said, with barely a tremor in my voice, "but smoking is not allowed in the hall."

"Yeah?" he said getting out his box of matches.

"But you are allowed to smoke in the other room," I said hopefully.

"Yeah?" he said removing match from box.

There was a breath-holding quietness in that hall.

"Oh please don't give me a hard time," said I with a helpless plea in my voice. "I have never done this before." Fortunately, appealing to his better nature was absolutely the way to go.

"Oh, come on," said his girlfriend. "We can smoke outside." He shrugged and followed her out. The held breath (mine especially) was released and people talked and danced again; the danger was over.

Now what of young Ali? He was not at all intimidated by the metal, leather, or hair—quite the contrary. He was used to seeing his brother and his brother's pals in similar gear. Whenever I looked his way he was happily playing with the big boys or lying sleepily on someone's lap. Eventually, however, utterly exhausted, he crawled onto the stage and wrapped himself very tightly around his brother's legs. Naturally, this greatly impeded Ramsey's performance. He tried to shake off the clinging encumbrance and move about the stage, dragging Ali around the floor while still singing into the mike. Intervention from Mother was clearly needed. As I approached the stage that "held-breath" quality was again in the air. I am sure I even heard boos and hisses, but undaunted, I pried the reluctant limpet from his brother's legs and carried him off the stage. He put his thumb in his mouth, his arms around my neck, and promptly fell asleep. The room relaxed.

I learned a lot that night at my first punk gig, and it has stayed with me all my days. I learned, as they say, not to judge a book by its cover or a man by his appearance. I learned that under all that black leather and metal and Doc Martens and Mohican haircuts, they are just lads. I no longer flinch and cross the road when I see them approaching, but smile confidently as I would to any other person I passed on the sidewalk. In fact, I smile more genuinely, and surprised, they always smile back.

And Ali had his own lesson to learn. Just a few weeks later it was Halloween, and lunchtime he came rushing home from school saying he needed "fancy dress" for that very afternoon. As good luck would have it, Ramsey was there and suggested Ali dress up as a punk. Ali protested very loudly that he was not dressing up "punk" as that is just what people wore every day! But time was short and punk gear was to hand. Complaining bitterly, he put on his brother's huge Docs, black leather jacket, and chains, and had his hair gelled to great heights. He looked terrific. And he won second prize—a much-valued Snickers bar. He was thrilled to bits, and so that day he also learned his lesson—that being a punk brings its own sweet rewards.

THE DICKS, PRIVATE OUTRAGE, THE CRUCIFUCKS, AND AFFLICTED

Mike Paré

I kept a journal from junior high until about halfway through my sophomore year of high school. The entries ended around 1986, when I was caught in a whirlwind of dubious teenage doings, and was too busy to write down even the smallest details. Below are the remains of an expedition into the hazy memories of my youth.
Journal Entry from 10/26/84:

"Went to my first show. Saw the Dicks, Private Outrage, the Crucifucks, and Afflicted."

That's all I wrote in my journal, and what I remember is still pretty vague. I remember a group of us got a ride to the show in the back of our buddy Andy Baptista's truck. It was late October, and it was freezing. We drove to a small community center somewhere in the East Bay, a little wood structure painted a leftover green. The lighting was bad. The crowd was around forty or fifty people, including the bands. But I remember it was amazing.

I have a strong memory of the Crucifucks—four really regular-looking, but weird guys. They looked like four creeps that just got off a bus somewhere, but they played the most fucked up music. With his small frame and long curly hair, the singer resembled Ronnie James Dio. But he sounded insane, his voice was really high pitched and whiney. And he was literally rabid, foaming at the mouth during his performance. I remember Andy got drooled on, standing too close to the stage. I thought they were amazing.

I also remember the Dicks—just a great, energized band, probably an early version of the post-Texas lineup. Gary Floyd was an impressive performer, bouncing all over the stage. Again, they were just basic looking guys wearing standard thrift store wares. The bands were all so weird, it really made me think about punk rock a lot differently. It wasn't just about being super punk and hardcore, it definitely wasn't about "cool stuff" like books or records, or even clothing. It made sense to me that it was more hardcore to just be a fucking weird person, or more basically, a person who was willing to question authority—and that meant all authority. That was hardcore enough. You didn't need tattoos, a bullet belt, or a mohawk to be hardcore. You just had to be a misfit.

What's clear from the short journal entry is the turn of events that follows—my life in the journal was previously occupied with girls, school, and social stuff. Then after the first show, life takes a turn and the journal becomes about a community of punks—a life of shows, parties, music, and petty crime. Teenage runaways. Drugs. Suicide, even. But it's also apparent that we had a community and our own ethics to live by if we chose to.

There was a code that said that when I saw someone who looked like a freak (which was a rare thing in the suburbs in 1984), I could become their friend without knowing them at all. I would fight to the death for them, this beautiful stranger at the bus stop, this gorgeous tanned punk girl wearing a DK shirt with the sleeves cut off...You left it at my house and I smelled that t-shirt forever—until that punk girl-smell was totally gone.

FUCK THE KNACK

Chris Rest

I remember the first time I saw a punk rocker was at The Knack concert in Isla Vista, about 1978. My mom took me to the concert. There was this guy with a leather jacket on with big white letters on the back that read "FUCK THE KNACK." I thought he was crazy. I learned later that he was one of the area's first and only punk rockers, and called himself Chris Syphilis. He was the singer for Santa Barbara's first punk band, the Strap On Dicks.

I didn't get into punk until a few years later. I think it was 1980. I was living in Carpinteria. My friends and I were in Jr. high and had been introduced to punk rock through an older neighbor whom we often surfed with. I think he was about sixteen at the time. The first three records we got were *Never Mind The Bollocks*, *Group Sex*, and *Damaged*. We also had a cassette of *Los Angeles*. We were the only three kids at our school that listened to punk. We all cut our hair and bought Converse "Chucks." We would buy button up shirts at the thrift store and write band names and skulls and such on them with permanent markers. I remember how much the ink smelled, even after the shirts had been washed. We tried our best to look like the skankin' cartoon guy on the back of the Circle Jerks record. One of the teachers at our school started calling us "The Clones" because we all pretty much looked and dressed the same. We used to play music in my bedroom and we called ourselves The Ratz, although in retrospect I think The Clones is a much better name.

My two friends went to their first show at Godzilla's in Los Angeles with their neighbor, Chuck, who had a driver's license and borrowed his mom's car. I think I was too scared to go or something. When they came back they told me of the adventure. It sounded amazing.

They told me about the "skank pit" and stage-dives and all the punkers in LA and the huge scene down there. About a month later we found out that D.O.A. was playing in Goleta, which was local. My mother and her boyfriend took me to the show. It was at the Goleta Community Center. I remember noticing the distinct smell of clove cigarettes when we arrived. I was amazed at how many punks were there.

I finally got the nerve to go into the pit. After one or two times around the circle, I took an elbow right in the nose—easy to do when your face is right at elbow level. My nose instantly started gushing blood. I just let it bleed all over my face and down the front of my shirt. I thought that was the punk thing to do. I remember the older punks looking at me, wide eyed... That made me feel good.

After that, my friends and I went to every show we possibly could, and acquired as much music as we could get our hands on. It was an awesome time.

LOSING MY PUNK ROCK VIRGINITY IN THE CHARM CITY

Stewart Ebersole

Punk found me at a time when I was a teenaged disaster. In 1980, Ronald Reagan took office. I was in eighth grade, 6 feet tall, lanky to the point of retarded, and wasn't horribly athletic—a fact that aggravated my father into a frenzy. On the social frontier I didn't fare much better. My face was so overwhelmed with acne that it was difficult to look at myself in the mirror, let alone ask a girl out on a date or anything like that. Sure, I had a few friends at school, but for the most part my life was looking rather shitty. The whole thing, the life, the looks, and the abilities were a fucking mess, and I had no idea how to change that.

I spent the next two years of my life "acting" punk, but for a kid growing up in the small, rural, farming town of Red Lion, PA, real punk influences were just not to be found. At the time, television portrayed punk as a rather violent culture, but from what I had learned up to that point, the mass media's picture of it was a bit distorted. It wasn't until I met a guy named George that my perception of the punk rock lifestyle changed dramatically.

George was my first punk rock mentor. He was about five years older than me, and was a classic early-80s "skate punk." He was a straight edge kid, who spent his teen years in the Washington, DC scene, and while helping him build his monstrous skateboard ramp, he would tell me stories of seeing shows in DC that both piqued my interest in that scene and seem totally impossible to comprehend. Something told me that by knowing and working with George my initiation into the punk subculture was going start moving very rapidly, and I was excited. Very, very excited!!!

The sum total of my show-going experience was the two or three times that I had gone to parties near the local college to see a band called Second Crisis (a local reggae-inspired punk band) play in basements and kitchens, but this still didn't seem quite punk to me. I knew that there was something more out there and so I kept searching for it. All of a sudden, I found it. One night while listening to 99.1 WHFS' concert calendar I heard that the Circle Jerks were playing at a small club in Baltimore called The Loft. So excited that I didn't know what to do, I called the radio station hoping to score directions, but was given just a street address, which was good enough for me.

The next day I asked my dad for directions, informed my friends of the news, told them my plan, and somehow we all got permission to go to the show. Guided by George, who was our seasoned professional, my friends John and Byron would accompany us to see a show at a club in a town that none of us had ever been to before. It was a scary thought, but it would turn out to be one of the most important experiences of my entire life.

It was a chilly November afternoon as the four of us loaded into my dad's 1979 conversion van and started driving toward a city just forty-five miles away. Everything that I was wearing under my green pin-clad army surplus trenchcoat was ripped to shreds. My mohawk was poorly spiked, and as I walked down our porch stairs, my mom was treating me as though I was heading off to do some trick-or-treating. I didn't know for sure, but I thought that I looked pretty punk rock. In retrospect, I looked pretty stupid, but I was just a kid and didn't really give a fuck.

The hour or so drive down to Baltimore was tense, and the entire way down we listened to George's array of punk tapes on a boom-box.

We were headed to our first big punk show outside of the greater York, Pennsylvania area and all that I really remember was the four of us in the van, the music, and the anticipation of making it to The Loft on time to see the show. The rest is all a blur; a total fucking blur.

I was excited and sick to my stomach as we neared the club...and fuck, like that we saw the line of punk rocker kids stretching around the block in front of a very sketchy looking three-story building. No matter what I was thinking on the drive down, seeing all of the kids with mo-hawks, shaved heads, leather jackets, trench-coats, and so on, made me feel like I was the most ill-prepared person in the entire world. No mat-ter, though... I had my friends and that was enough to keep me focused on the show.

George gave us the pep-talk as we parked and walked to the club. He mentioned that "the pit" was not a violent place and that we should respect that. Don't start fights, and help people up when they fall down..! This was the first time that I had ever heard words like this come out of George's mouth. His stories were often filled with bloody torment in the pit and stage-dives turning into broken necks, and now he was encouraging us to be boy-scouts. Fuck, that sure didn't sound Punk to me. But I listened and well, it was some pretty good advice back in those days when a lot of people found their way into the "circle storm."

It took us nearly thirty minutes to make our way through the line and into the club, and I could feel my fright turning into frenzy. From the alley way leading to the door of the club I could hear the dull roar of voices inside, accompanied by the music being played through the PA system. I can remember singing along at times; banging my head and fist in unison to the 30 second anthems. Finally, I handed the man at the door my five dollars and made the right turn into the club. It was at that very moment that my life was changed—virtually in an instant—forever.

It became immediately apparent that the show had been over adver-tised, and apparently, this was the first big show in this new space. By the time my little crew entered the space, it was obvious to me that if every person that was in line with us, along with those already inside, were to be allowed in, well, there would be some serious overcrowding.

The space itself was already hot and steamy from all of the kids just standing around talking, smoking, making out, or whatever, and it was only half-filled. As more and more people arrived, we found our way over to the wall where George laid out the list of things "not to do" in the pit or to other people, and in order to ensure our safety.

For the most part, I was overwhelmed because I had never seen anything like this and I worried that I might just have a very difficult time navigating this new social scene. However, in no time flat, bands and third-tier promoters in the club were handing me fliers for upcoming Baltimore and DC shows...about one every minute or so. Never before had it been so easy to simply walk up and begin talking to kids (even though they looked very scary) and make new friends. Apparently, most of us came from similar social backgrounds (freaks, geeks, losers, and misfits in our respective high schools), and so everybody there seemed to be able to relate to everybody else that was there. This was the exact social scene that I had been searching for, for nearly three years, and now I was an active part of it.

The show was slated to start at 9 pm, and Reptile House was the first band to play that night. As I would come to find out very soon, they were a very popular Baltimore band and had a huge following of very dedicated fans. As soon as the guitar player strummed the first chord, Daniel Higgs, the singer, appeared and the entire crowd was pressed tight up on the stage singing along with songs that they apparently knew very well.

I watched George as he made his way into the developing pit. He danced in a strange way that we would refer to as "opening the sunroof," whereby he would creep around low to the floor spinning his arm around in a circle as though he was opening a twist-to-open car sunroof. I didn't really understand the mechanics of this new dance, but next thing that I know I am fighting my way into the pit to emulate his strange style with some poor results. Surprisingly, the circle pit, while looking dangerous, was actually rather gentle. I got pushed and thrown around with great frequency, and found myself being picked up by fellow dancers more than I was actually dancing. More than anything else, within a few minutes of this, I was really, really tired. And, with one quick push to the front of the crowd, I found myself standing close to the stage to watch the rest of the band's performance.

Many times, across the throngs of people jumping off the stage, Mr. Higgs would pull himself out onto the crowd by grasping people's hair, and lunging with one leg out and onto those unlucky enough to be compressed against the stage. He did this frequently, and between him and those pesky stage-divers, I (being the tallest kid in the crowd) was getting the shit kicked out of me. At one point, I ducked to avoid being landed upon by one leather jacket-clad kid that seemed to dominate the stage, and fell to the ground where I was getting trampled by what seemed to be everybody.

When a hand grabbed me by the hair and pulled me to my feet, I found out it was Daniel Higgs doing the pulling (how fucking cool is that…?). Upon getting me to my feet, he used my head of hair to pull himself out onto the crowd once more. So, not only was I at this amazing show, watching this amazingly strange band, but I was "part of the show" to boot. This was just unprecedented in my life—having only ever seen bigger bands play in stadiums prior to this point, it just seemed so natural for me to fall in love with it.

I don't know how long Reptile House played, nor do I remember much of what they sounded like, but "This will be our last song. Thank you for listening" signaled the impending intermission. I danced through the last song, and when it was over and the fluorescent house lights were turned on, everybody let out a collective roar of approval.

Intermission lasted the best part of thirty minutes, and in that time we learned that the Grimm would not be playing due to van troubles. The Circle Jerks would be the next band to play, which meant that if everything went right, I would be home before my 1 am curfew and my parents would be very happy.

After mingling and making plans to come to Baltimore for future shows with my friend John, the lights fell and the Circle Jerks took the stage. We all gathered at the same place along the wall, and as soon as the band started the first song a huge pit began to form, bodies were flying off the stage two and three at a time, and I was a bit nervous again. I realized that night that I wasn't such a good dancer, and I was a sitting duck if I stood near the stage, so for a long time I stood by the wall and just watched the show.

A few minutes passed and suddenly, out of nowhere, I see George climb onto the stage, dance around a little bit, and then jump off into a sea of hands. I wanted to do it. It looked so awesome but, fuck, in the face of the mayhem I was still scared half to death. Finally, after much deliberation, I decided to join in on the fun.

I fought my way into the pit, danced for a few seconds, made my way to the opposing corner of the stage, and there I stood with the hopes of not getting kicked in the face by a stray combat boot again. And when the chance arose I would pump my fist and scream lyrics as the microphone was pushed out into the crowd by the absolutely crazy singer, Keith Morris.

A frantic front-man, Keith would jump off the bass drum, off the monitors, off amplifiers, and off people's heads. He would shake up beers and fire them into the crowd, and he would throw people off of the stage if they lingered too long. He would spit into the crowd and invite the crowd to spit on the band, and then he would attack you, both verbally and physically, if you did so. In all, his antics were so playfully brutal that I was actually scared to be near the stage. But, no matter what my fear of Keith Morris was, I wanted so badly to climb up on stage and sing along—or even stage-dive—but I was pretty much a pussy at this point in the show.

George jumped up on stage when "Red Tape," his favorite CJ song, started. He ran over to me, pulled me up onto the stage, and I was a deer-in-the-headlights. I had absolutely no idea what to do. I was lost. I was panicking. In a last ditch effort, I mimicked the "sunroof" dance as best as I could, waited for the chorus, "Killing me Killing you, Red Tape, Red Tape," and sang into Keith's microphone, while he pulled my hair and my face right beside his, as he screamed the chorus. Then he grabbed me and threw me off of the stage. To my amazement, the crowd not only caught my lanky frame, but they carried me around for a few seconds before I simply ran out of hands and fell straight onto the ground on my back. I was picked up very fast by concerned punks that I didn't know, and I just thought that this was the best experience ever.

For the rest of the show I perfected my abilities climbing onto the stage, dancing around, and jumping into the crowd. George commented on our drive home that I spent more time on top of the crowd than I probably should have, but he said it in a joking tone, and so I didn't take it to personally. From that point on I was a frequent flier from the stages of many punk rock shows where I was an attendee, and it all started there at that show in Baltimore. Strangely, I still do it on occasion…!

Forty-five minutes later the Circle Jerks were finished with a blazing set and two encores, and it was nearing 12:30 in the morning. We walked out the door, down the alley, and onto the street, and I had left a lot of my life back in that dingy little space and couldn't wait to come back to be part of another show.

As we walked toward the car, it started snowing. In fact, if my memory serves me, there was already about an inch on the ground, because my people and me were making and throwing little snowballs at each other and our new friends as we walked to the car.

I fumbled through my pockets and found my keys (thinking that I may have lost them in the pit for just a second), unlocked the doors, and started the engine. We were off. For the first few minutes we were all silent. I was sweating so badly that my shirt had nearly frozen on the walk to the car. We smelled bad. Once on the highway, however, the entire van erupted in laughter and chatter. Each and every person in the van obviously had a great time (even George, who had been going to punk rock shows for two or three years at that point). We told tales of our discovery, bravery, and our "trial by fire" into the strange world of punk rock. There was no hesitation to state that we were finally real PUNK ROCKERS, and would remain so for years to come.

That night we all made it home safely. The next morning I woke up and I tried to explain to my parents about how much fun I had and how I couldn't wait to go back but, well...they were my parents and they had doubts about me turning into a PUNK ROCKER on their watch. Many times they cut me off or chuckled when I told them about the dancing, the stage-diving, the bands, and the camaraderie that I experienced that night, and their apparent lack of concern only solidified my desires to return to the community of people that treated me like gold and changed the way that I saw the world in just one evening of music and fun.

While it initially did not sit so well with my parents, they began to treat my weekend sojourns to Baltimore as nothing special. Their later support, and the support of my new friends in Baltimore, kept me returning to that space just about every weekend for the three years of its existence.

It has now been nearly twenty-five years since I attended my first Punk show, and since that time, I have basically committed my life to the ideals of community and volunteerism that were important lessons that I learned from the early-American punk rock scene. It has been a long and hard-fought battle, but I still refer to myself as an overgrown punk kid every time I am forced to describe myself, and I suspect I will continue to do this for the rest of my life. Even today, when I am talking to old-head punk kids about their involvement, the statements, "Punk rock changed my life" and "I am still giving back to the community that gave everything to me" sum up our collective experiences pretty well.

In a life where kids now treat punk rock as just a "stage" in their lives, I think that it would be really hard for me to convince them that punk rock—or at least its vast history—is far from just a "stage" or a "music choice," and so I generally don't feel the need to get on my soapbox and begin my discourse. This is possibly the greatest shame of all: that our collective stories may amount only to remembrances of elder-states-punks, never again to be experienced by an entire generation. So, in retrospect... THANK YOU BALTIMORE, JULES, THE LOFT, and every band, person and experience that you gave to me in this lifetime. You changed my fucking life...!

A BASSOON AND A CHAINSAW

Al Quint

I didn't really get to go to any concerts or shows until I started my freshman year at Boston University in 1978. It wasn't as though I was forbidden to attend shows, but my parents didn't encourage it and I didn't have any friends to go with, anyway. During the summer before starting college, I did go with a friend to a concert at the old Twin Rinks hockey arena in Danvers, MA that had a bunch of hard rock bands. The first of these bands, Revolver, opened with Thin Lizzy's "The Boys Are Back In Town." The Nervous Eaters, who were a punk band, were the headliners, but it was running late and we were long gone by then.

So when I got to BU, I needed to make a pilgrimage to the Boston punk mecca, The Rat, which I did with the same friend, who was visiting one weekend in the fall. My dorm was only a few blocks from Kenmore Square, where the club was located. But that wasn't my first punk show, either. The headliners were this godawful bar rock band The Stompers.

They were more Springsteen than Sex Pistols and appealed to the Boston rock 'n' roll audience who didn't really embrace the harder-edged punk sounds. The Stompers later ended up on a major label and you can probably find their albums for 99 cents somewhere.

The first punk show I *did* attend was in January of 1979 and it was at The Rat. A few weeks later, I attended my first punk rock concert...hell the first concert I'd attended period and that was with the Clash. Not a bad introduction, eh? When I got back to BU for my second semester, I noticed that there were posters all around Kenmore and other parts of the city advertising the Plasmatics' debut single "Butcher Baby," and it also had a date for when they'd be playing at The Rat. I'd actually heard "Butcher Baby" on one of the college stations and taped it off the radio. I decided I needed to go to that show and experience honest-to-goodness live punk rock. Picking up the 7" just before the show added further inspiration, even though the live tracks on the b-side were kind of substandard.

The night of the show arrived, which was a Sunday. It was snowing and there was maybe two inches on the ground. I couldn't find anyone else on the floor of the Warren Towers dorm where I resided to go with me, and I wasn't friendly with the smattering of punk-type people I'd seen at BU. Actually, that's not true. There was a punk fan named Jim Coffman who lived on the same floor and had good musical taste. Jim later left BU and booked the Underground club for a few years, and also managed Mission of Burma and the Neats. He's still involved in the music business after all these years. Anyway, Jim had moved to another dorm, so I couldn't ask him.

I trudged through the snow to the club by myself. I didn't know anyone there. I was eighteen years old—the drinking age was eighteen at that point—ah, the good old days. The Rat was dank and seedy, living up to its notorious reputation. It was filled with smoke, the smell of stale beer and various miscreants. There was a slight sense of danger, but not to the point where I wanted to run back to Warren Towers or my house in the cozy suburb of Swampscott. Besides, I'd already been there for that Stompers show...but this was definitely a different crowd. Since I still lacked any sort of social skills and some of the other attendees did seem intimidating, I kept to myself.

The Plasmatics were playing that night with the Molls, who were more of an art punk band. They had an electric bassoon player and a keyboard player, in addition to the standard guitar/bass/drums. I remember being moderately intrigued, especially one song towards the end, a speedy roar called "White Stains" that ended up on a 7" that I picked up that spring. After the Molls' set, there were video clips being shown on TV monitors around the club, including a few conceptual videos featuring the Plasmatics—"Fast Food Service" and "Concrete Shoes." When the latter video ended, the lights went up on the stage and there they were. It was a sonic blast I hadn't experienced before, introducing itself with all the subtlety of a thunder clap—the three musicians wailing away, and in the middle of the storm, Ms. Wendy O. Williams, wearing a blood-stained Plasmatics shirt tight enough to emphasize you-know-what and see through black nylon panties. She bumped and grinded, and would pull away just in time when men would attempt to grope her. Wendy definitely had the moves—no doubt perfected by her experience performing in live sex shows in Times Square.

The songs went by in a high-speed blur. I can't remember what the others were wearing, but do know that they donned fast food hats when they got to "Fast Food Service." The climax (no pun intended), of course, was "Butcher Baby." For that song, a guitar on a rack was brought out, ready for its chainsaw sacrifice. An electric violinist wearing a hood sawed away, and Wendy held up the saw of destruction, then proceeded to cut through it with skillful ease. That was the end of the set. In those days, the bands would play two sets each but I figured I'd seen what I came for and called it a night.

As for the Clash concert, I know this is technically my second show, but it also left an indelible impression. After being blown away by their first album, the various singles and the recently released "Give 'Em Enough Rope," I was excited to find out they'd be playing the Harvard Square Theater in February. Tickets went on sale at the Strawberries record store and I purchased one for the princely sum of $7.50. It's a good thing I did, because the show sold out quickly. Once again, I went solo got there really early. Waiting to go in, I saw all the leather-festooned punks, and didn't feel as though I fit in, so didn't attempt a conversation with anyone. Those feelings dissipated once the show began, plus I ran into Jim, so at least there was *one* person I could talk to. A local garage-type band, The Rentals, opened and pretty much got booed off the stage (they weren't *that* bad, though). Bo Diddley followed—yeah, *that* Bo Diddley—and he had the crowd eating out of his hand by the end of the set.

He got asked back for an encore and blew a kiss to the audience while the shave 'n a haircut shuffle got cooking again.

Then it was time for the Clash. A multi-nation flag tapestry dropped to the accompaniment of "There's A Riot Going On," and the band charged the stage and broke into "I'm So Bored With USA." By the time they got to "Tommy Gun," I was up from my seat in the balcony, pumping my fist away. I also remember their tour shirts were $6, but I didn't like the style, so I passed. I did get a cool Clash tour pin, which I still own to this day.

I never did go to see the Plasmatics play again, and didn't see the Clash again until the "Combat Rock" tour in '82, both to my regret. Still, it's a testament to the impact of both shows that I can vividly remember the details of each night and that created the hunger for the live experience—whether in a club, arena, or (preferably) a basement or hall space—that I still crave to this day.

I USED TO DO ACID

Joe Queer

My first punk show? Shit that was a lot of brain cells ago. I mean, I was going to see bands at The Rat in the late-70s. The Rat was Boston's answer to CBGB's. Beantown back then was going through an uneasy time where most of the bands still had long hair and looked like rockers, not punks, though that would change soon. After a while we started seeing new wave bands with stupid skinny ties and shiny boots. You knew a few years before all these new wavers had been into Jethro Tull and The Eagles, but doing the new wave thing meant they didn't have to get too down and dirty. To me, they were all phonies; their offspring would gratefully embrace ska a few years later. Ska and new wave were for all the losers too scared to be into punk rock. Yeah, I like The Bosstones, Op Ivy, Madness, and a few others, but all the rest sucked. I mean, me and all my pals wanted to be like Johnny Thunders or DeeDee Ramone or Iggy Pop, all fucked up on drugs day and night—not the damn trombone player for Reel Big Fish who looked, talked, and acted like our parent's accountant—fuck that shit. I saw everyone there from the Dead Boys to the DK's to The Police.

The Police played to about forty-seven people on a Tuesday or Wednesday night, and the only reason I even went was because our pals in The Vinny Band were opening up. At the time, I smoked weed, and I went up to Stewart Copeland and Andy Summers and asked them if they wanted to get high. They both said "hell yeah" and we went out in front of the club and smoked a joint. I asked them if the other guy (Sting) wanted to smoke too, and they both laughed and said no—he's high enough on his own, thank you. They played, and even back then, Sting was full of himself; except for the fact they were a touring band from the UK, he probably would have got his ass kicked for being a pompous motherfucker. That type didn't go over well with the locals at The Rat back in those days.

I remember seeing bottles thrown at bands when they were deemed unworthy by the locals, and on occasion even getting punched as they were loading their gear out the back door—and by girls too!! My drummer Hugh's girlfriend was Nikki Jerret—her sister, Alyssa, was married to Joe Perry from Aerosmith—and those two were a pair that would beat a full house. When they were in a club you knew it. Nikki was not above throwing a bottle or two at a lame band, and I quickly learned to just keep playing and avoid any stage banter cause that was just asking to be insulted by her and her cronies. You'd be taking a quick break after what you thought was your best song and Nikki would start screaming "Turn down the vocals" at the top of her lungs. Kind of killed the moment as they say, but I learned a lot there. I miss those days if only because of the honesty. I mean, if your band sucked you got an instant review from the audience, which was comprised of every form of drug addict, unemployable loser, and onanist Boston had to offer. They may have been the dregs of society, but they did not suffer fools gladly.

I'll tell you about one show my old singer, Wimpy Rutherford, and I went to back in those days. This was just business as usual for us, but for some reason, it still sticks out in my mind. Wimpy and I were driving around Portsmouth, NH one Sunday afternoon trying to decide whether to go to Boston to see our favorite band in those days—The Real Kids—play a matinee. We figured out we had enough dough and started off. I casually mentioned I had two hits of blotter acid some kid had given me at work. Wimpy immediately came out of his pot-induced coma, which he was always in, and told me he'd do a hit if I would. Knowing a good thing when I saw one, I immediately whipped the stuff out of my wallet and down the hatch it went. This was about 2 pm and doors were at 3. It's an hour drive to Boston, so we took the acid and headed straight down.

We made it to the club ok, but doors weren't open yet so we had to wait out in the parking lot. We both started getting fucked up and paranoid as we looked at the freaks with green hair standing outside the club. This was fucking 1978, and people like that still seemed weird to us at the time. Nowadays everyone's a punk, but back then it meant something, and if you had green hair it took some balls. Anyway, we were starting to get high as hell and were all worried about getting out of the car and into the club. We double- and triple-checked to make sure we had the keys, our money, and IDs. Finally, we made the move, got out, locked the doors, and started walking over to the club. Some girls in a car next to us beeped their horn, but we ignored them. They rolled their window down and yelled at us to stop. We fought the urge to make a run for it, and turned around to see what they wanted. They asked if we were going to lock our car and we said we did—at which point they said, "Well, you left your windows down." Wow. We were so concerned with locking up, we hadn't noticed. We tried to act nonchalant like we meant to do it and attempted to laugh. As to my laugh I really can't tell you, but Wimpy sounded like a hyena in pain. We rolled the windows up and went into the club.

Once inside we stood with our backs to the wall and just stared at people trying not to scream for help. At one point, we looked at each other, and Wimpy said, "Let's get the fuck out of here cause I'm freaking out," so we bailed after staying inside for about ten minutes. Wimpy completely lost it, and insisted we drive back to NH as he couldn't handle one more minute of that freak show. I wanted to stay, but in my condition, couldn't offer much of a reason besides the fact we paid to get in, and since Wimpy was my ride, I didn't have much choice.

We got out on the Southeast Expressway and immediately hit a traffic jam. Wimpy started really freaking out, saying he couldn't handle it and he wanted to get out of the car and start running. Where he wanted to run wasn't really discussed, but he felt it was the thing to do. I told him this was no time for a jog and he just stared straight ahead, every so often muttering "I'm freaking out" under his breath. This was rather disconcerting as he was driving, but back in those days I took this sort of stuff in stride. Finally, the traffic started moving, and we approached the Tobin Bridge where we had to pay a fifty cent toll. Wimpy hadn't said a word for five minutes, and right when we were getting to the toll booth he announced that he was "peaking." We got the toll paid somehow and drove over the bridge to Chelsea where he pulled over at a closed gas station and ran out of the car behind the place. I just sat there expecting him to come back, but after five minutes he hadn't shown up, so I went to find him.

He was leaning up against the back of the building-spread eagled, eyes closed, and panting loudly. I watched him for a bit, but he never moved. Finally I went up to him and tapped him on the shoulder. He jumped up and let out a little yell and said, "I ain't driving—you have to." I dragged him back to the car and started driving. He told me that the acid was "right on top of me" and that he couldn't control his arms and legs. He was slowly going into the fetal position and he couldn't stop his body from doing it.

At this stage of the ballgame, I was starting to laugh as I had seen him get fucked up, but never this badly. Sure enough, as I drove, his body started curling up and he had to put his hands under his thighs to stop his arms from curling up. He was all hunched up, trying in vain to stop curling into a ball, when his voice started going and he couldn't talk. You ever see that *Three Stooges* episode where they eat alum and start talking all fucked up? Well, that is exactly how Wimpy started talking. Oh man, it was funny as hell, and when I asked if I should tell Dianne—his girlfriend at the time—about him doing acid, he practically had a convulsion shaking his head no, as he couldn't do anything but mutter. He made me pull over on I-95 and said he had to get out of the car. He backed out and had his knees on the ground and arms on the seat, and stared at me and would not move. We somehow made it back home where he came down enough to announce that he wanted to drive back to the show—we actually made it in time to see The Real Kids. Going to see a show back then was like joining the army: always an adventure.

The Rat was fun, though. You'd always see Rik Ocasek or Jonathan Richman or some famous dude at shows. The Ramones went there a few times after they got done with their own show over on Lansdowne Street. I remember going with the Ramones to The Rat after we had opened up for them once, and the stupid jock doorman not letting Joey in because he didn't have an ID. Jimmy Harold, the owner, came down and screamed, "Don't you know who this is you moron? It's Joey Ramone!! Now get the fuck outta here—you're fired!" I wish I'd filmed that little episode.

I got up the balls to go up to Jonathan Richman once, and I told him I liked his song "New England." He just stared at me, and after a few seconds said, "Thank you, thank you very much." Odd doesn't begin to describe him, though he did tell me once to always remember to write for the little girls. I always liked that advice.

The Real Kids opened up for The Troggs once at a small club called Cantones. There were about ninety people there, tops. I was standing between John Felice of The Real Kids, and Jonathan Richman, watching The Troggs do "Wild Thing," and thinking that it doesn't get much cooler than this. Of course, The Troggs aren't a punk rock band but they completely kicked ass, and to this day it's still one of the top five shows I have ever been to in my life. John Felice, to me, was a rock god and wrote killer tunes.

When The Real Kids were on, they were the best band in town, though a bigger collection of goofballs you'd be hard put to find. Alpo, the bass player, could be a real asshole. I went up to him once at The Rat and told him I was psyched to see his band, and he just screamed "Fuck you, faggot" in my face, which precluded any more conversation. I became friends with him later (some free Percocets softened him up and paved the way to an uneasy friendship).

I recall seeing Felice doing an acoustic set at The Rat; he was wearing jeans ripped in the crotch and his ballsack was hanging out. The whole crowd was cracking up, and of course, he was oblivious. Billy Borgioli, the guitar player, looked exactly like Caroline Kennedy—so you know what he was called. Howie, the drummer, was great, but couldn't really hold a conversation. Yeah, The Real Kids were great.

Cheetah Chrome, of The Dead Boys, was living in town for a few years and we would get all fucked up and go to our rehearsal spot and play Rolling Stones songs. I remember stopping in the middle of "Live With Me," and begging him to let me sing because he was so off-key. The whole scene was fueled on drugs and booze, and you would no more think of turning down a line of coke than jumping in front of a freight train. It was just the way everyone operated back then and there was a great sort of energy that I loved. It wasn't a career move to be in a punk band then. It was either "Welcome to Burger King, may I take your order?" or punk rock. No in-between.

I guess maybe I should have written about seeing Minor Threat or the DK's but the late-70s was when I started seeing punk shows at The Rat. The Real Kids, DMZ, The Thrills, The Nervous Eaters, The Neighborhoods, Willy Alexander and the Boom Boom Band...those were my favorite bands and really the first punk shows I went to. Gang Green, The FU's, Straw Dogs would all come later. I heard Black Flag and the DK's and started getting into harder stuff, and started my own band, but these are my roots and where I got into seeing punk rock bands live.

AUTHOR BIOS

Michael Azerrad

Author, *Our Band Could Be Your Life: Scenes from the American Indie Underground 1981–1991* (Little, Brown, 2001).

David Alan Boisineau

Born in '74, the youngest of five kids, and grew up in the suburbs of Richmond, VA. Encouraged and supported by my parents to be my own person. Have been skateboarding since I was five or six, and drawing and painting longer than that. I've now been tattooing for eleven years. My lifelong enemies are cops, jocks, and born-again christians.

Scott Bourne

Originally from North Carolina, Scott has spent the last ten years traveling the world as a well-known professional skateboarder and is admired across the industry for his uncompromising work ethic and his caustic integrity. He currently resides in Paris, where he is simultaneously editing his first novel and working on his second. His writing has been featured in magazines both inside and outside of skateboarding, and he has penned a column for *Slap* for a number of years. He is currently making the rounds of Europe to promote a book and film project executed in Mongolia in 2005, as well as a book of poetry entitled *Cheating on the Metronome*, set for release in the latter part of '07. When he is not at his desk typing on his ol' Corona, he will most likely be found wandering the City of Light in search of the words that cause a man to write. As the French would say, *Si il n'existait pas, il aurait fallu l'inventer.*

Anna Brown

Anna Brown was born and raised in Berkeley, CA. She was a member of the notorious all-girl gang The Twisted Dog Sisters.

Sto Cinders

Sto grew up in Alexandria, VA, where the nearby Washington, DC punk scene saved him from being a sad and lonely loser. He remembers fondly the Beehive Collective, the 9:30 Club on F Street, the first Black Cat, the Safari Club, St. Stephens Church, Wilson Center, Mountain Lodge on M Street, the American Legion Hall, (getting maced at the) Betapunk warehouse, Club Soda, Happy Hardcore House, and Go Records. He now lives in Brooklyn where he makes art and runs Cinders Gallery: www.cindersgallery.com. This story takes place in 1991, the year punk broke.

Craigums

Name: Craigums

Past: All You Can Eat, Your Mother, What Happens Next?, Colbom, This Is My Fist, Love Songs, etc...

Present: Professional Air Guitarist

Future: Eat some pizza, ride my bike, go to (another) punk show

Paul Curran

Paul Curran, a recent Coordinator of *Maximum Rocknroll* magazine, formerly of many bands such as Crimpshrine, Monsula, Go Sailor, and Shotwell. Currently, I'm in the bands Onion Flavored Rings and Surrender, and am still at *MRR* doing reviews, a monthly column, and coordinating MRR Radio.

Blag Dahlia

Blag Dahlia is a Rock Legend. A founding member of the Dwarves, record producer, songwriter, and author, his latest novel is called *NINA*. Check out more at: www.thedwarves.com.

Chris Duncan

Chris Duncan spent his formative years in the state that birthed Bruce Springsteen and the Misfits. Like so many folks from the era of polo shirts, co-opted surf culture, and heavy metal, he found solace in riding a skateboard and inevitably, in hardcore-punk music. For the better part of a decade, he went to shows up and down the east coast from DC to Boston. In 1995, Chris migrated west to northern California, where he resides today. Chris is a visual artist, co-publisher (along with Griffin McPartland) of the art-based zine *Hot and Cold*, and father of a very amazing little girl. His knees hurt way too much to skateboard anymore and he will probably lose his hair any minute now. *My First Time* is his first book.

Stewart Ebersole

Stewart Dean Ebersole lives in Philadelphia, PA making a living doing all kinds of creative stuff. Principally a geologist, at least by training, Stewart has found his niche in the wonderful world of design. He's a twenty-five year veteran of the American punk rock scene. Having played and toured with bands such as Railhed, Ambassador 990, and Hope and Anchor, he has recently given up hope in "the kids" and handed controls of the movement over to its new owners: Hot Topic, Urban Outfitters, and MTV, who are doing a fantastic job of eliminating punk rock's bite, while simultaneously hyping its rather weak bark. Stewart loves his family, his bicycles, his cats Frannie and Hades, cooking, and he still claims that DEVO changed his life—though he is not quite sure how exactly. You can contact Stewart at stewart.dean.ebersole@gmail.com because he loves email too.

Rob Fish

Robert Fish/Rasaraja: At the age of thirteen he took to the punk scene. The aggression and discontent within the music connected with him and he spent most Sundays at CBGB's, with his fake ID in hand, and the rest of the weekend attending shows around the NY tri-state area, skateboarding, and getting in as much trouble as possible. He took quickly to straight edge, vegetarianism, and Gaudiya Vaisnavism. Robert recorded his first record at fifteen, went on his first tour at sixteen, and since then has played in several bands (Release, Ressurection, 108, and The Judas Factor) which allowed him to travel around the world extensively. Over the years, he has released over eighteen records, played in nineteen countries, and forty-eight states. Currently, Robert is a district manager for the world's largest retail print provider and lives in Northern California with his wife and two kids, and continues to write and tour with 108.

Bull Gervasi

Bull Gervasi is a musician, community activist, and founding member of the Cabbage Collective in Philadelphia.

Joseph A. Gervasi

Joseph A. Gervasi went on to co-found (along with his brother Bull and Chris Fry) the Cabbage Collective, a DIY group that hosted all-ages shows in Philadelphia throughout the 1990s. He later co-founded Exhumed Films (www.ExhumedFilms) and is the co-owner of Diabolik DVD (www.DiabolikDVD.com). He lives in Philadelphia with some cats and a mortgage. Joseph can be reached at: DeadStare4Life@hotmail.com or through the Diabolik DVD website.

Harrison Haynes

Harrison Haynes was born and currently lives in Durham, NC. In 1996, he received a BFA in painting from the Rhode Island School of Design and since then has exhibited his work in group and solo shows in Los Angeles, New York, Washington, DC, and London. He is a co-founder of Branch Gallery and the drummer for the New York-based band, Les Savy Fav.

George Hurchalla

Born in 1966 in West Palm Beach, FL, went to high school in Florida and college in Pennsylvania. After spending four years as a punk radio DJ and graduating from Swarthmore College with a Mechanical Engineering degree in 1988, I studiously avoided engineering and set out to adventure the world, working odd jobs everywhere I traveled— from picking fruit in Australia to bungee jump videographer in Tahoe—before committing to a life of abject poverty (writing and photography). The *Encyclopedia Britannica* said in 1946 of my heritage that the "romantic national calling of the Slovaks is that of itinerant broombinders," and I set no higher purpose for myself for many years.

In late 2004, I launched the inflammatory "Bush Is Torture" campaign, inspired by the work of Minor Threat drummer Jeff Nelson, who screen printed "Meese Is A Pig" posters and t-shirts in Washington, DC in the mid-80s. In 2005, I published *Going Underground: American Punk 1979–1992*, which was started while working an excruciatingly dull job as a gatehouse security guard in Lake Tahoe, in 1998. A second edition was released in February 2006. Presently, I am working on a book on three decades of punk rock women.

Ann Kanaan

Ann Kanaan is a retired academic, but still active as a mother of three sons, one of whom is part owner of a nightclub which is always in need of bouncers. She believes she can see, there, the possibility of a new career.

Scott Kelly

Scott Kelly is a member of Neurosis.

Shawna Kenney

Shawna Kenney is the author of *Imposters* (Mark Batty Publisher) and *I Was a Teenage Dominatrix* (Last Gasp). She grew up in the Washington, DC area and contributes regularly to *Swindle* magazine.

Jillian Lauren

Jillian Lauren attends the MFA program at Antioch University. Her stories have been published in *Pindeldyboz* magazine, *Opium* magazine, the *Chiron Review*, and in the anthology *Pale House: A Collective*. She is currently working on a novel. She lives in Los Angeles with her husband, bass player Scott Shriner.

Rusty Mahakian

Rusty Mahakian is a writer, a stand up comic, and lives with his wife in Oakland, CA. Rusty is currently working as a stevedore at the Port of Oakland.

Sean McGhee

Sean McGhee was born in 1964 in West Cumbria in the North of England. He discovered the delights of the punk rock rebellion in 1977, joining his first and only band, Psycho Faction in early 1979, after compiling a punk fanzine, *Defused*, early the same year with his brothers.

Psycho Faction shared the stage with many of anarcho-punk's name acts (Crass, Flux, Poison Girls, Conflict, etc.) before calling it a day in 1984.

Latterly, Sean edited the internationally-read, eclectic magazine *Rock'n'Reel*, that he founded and published from 1988 until 2002. More recently he compiled the acclaimed series of four anarcho-punk compilations on Overground Records, and several offshoots from the albums. He also writes online and occasionally in print, covering punk in all its colours; handles publicity for bands, festivals, and events in a wide range of musical styles; and is attempting to learn more than three chords. Nowadays he edits the newly relaunched *Rock'n'Reel* magazine: www.rock-n-reel.co.uk.

Kyle Metzner

Kyle Metzner is a writer living in Oakland, CA. He is currently working with top physicists to discover a wormhole to the 9:30 Club, circa 1985.

Rebecca Miller

Rebecca Miller is a California native that likes to involve herself with most things literary and musical. For the past ten years she has been showing her artwork locally and internationally. She has recently begun to teach animation at the community school of art and music.

Mike Paré

Mike Paré is a visual artist from Northern California who currently lives in Brooklyn, NY. He played in hardcore bands in the mid-1980s (Rabid Lassie and Corporate Death), and put on a punk show in Livermore, CA at the age of fifteen. His artwork has been exhibited throughout the United States and Europe.

Jesse Pires

Manager, Arts and Culture Programs
International House Philadelphia

3701 Chestnut St.
Philadelphia, PA 19104
(ph) 215.895.6546
(fax) 215.895.6562
www.ihousephilly.org

John Poddy

John Poddy has been involved with many locally prominent Los Angeles bands, most notably as founding member of the influential band the Hags, who released one critically panned, but fanatically loved album before their ultimate demise. Mr. Poddy next formed Fag Rabbit, whose one release, the *Stone Man, Glass Woman*, featured the local fan favorite song "Happy and Drunk." Mr. Poddy was also a member of LA's ultimate "fun rock" band, The Caltransvestites, whose interview in *Flipside* magazine's 100th issue was the magazine's first full color feature. Other credits include a brief stint with the pioneering punk rock band U.X.A., appearing on a recording of the song "Pro Choice," which was included on a compilation recording which benefited the National Organization for Women (N.O.W.), as well as playing trumpet for LA's premier swing punk ensemble The Abe Lincoln Story. Mr. Poddy also collaborated on the closing credit song, "Don't Fuck with the Dead" for the Garrett Clancy film *Dead 7*. Mr. Poddy is currently playing with Smogtown.

Joe Queer

Joe Queer has been the leader of The Queers for over twenty years. For a guy that does not suffer fools gladly he seems to have surrounded himself with a lot of them.

Al Quint

From the time I had my red transistor radio when I was four years old, I've never lost my love for rock 'n' roll. It started with The Beatles, Rolling Stones, and Animals in the mid-60s, moved on to Chicago, Guess Who, The Who, Raspberries, and Elton John in the late-60s/early-70s, moved into hard rock and metal, with the likes of Aerosmith, Bad Company, Foghat, Blue Öyster Cult, AC/DC, and Ted Nugent. My sheltered, mainly friendless, suburban adolescence was largely spent in my room, alone, listening to records, and it got me through those years. The punk rock baptism came in 1977, courtesy of a high school classmate/college radio DJ. The Sex Pistols' "God Save The Queen" was the conversion experience and I've never looked back since then. The '77 punk era and the early-80s hardcore era are my lifelong inspiration.

Punk and hardcore stoked the already-planted seed of alienation and reinforced a refusal to conform, when I realized that what I was taught in college was a fuck of a lot different than the real world. I found solace in the anger and energy of those loud, fast sounds and it provided the impetus to start writing about it. I started a zine called *Suburban Punk* (known as *Suburban Voice* since the eleventh issue), and later on, started my own radio show, *Sonic Overload*. It also provided the impetus to take control of my life—taking Negative Approach's "why be something that you're not?" to heart. Some thirty years after hearing the Pistols, Clash, Damned, et al, high energy music remains my lifeline, my passion, and something I can't live without.

Jack Rabid

Jack Rabid is the founder, editor, and publisher of the respected semi-annual music magazine *The Big Takeover* (1980–present), and has written regularly for many other publications, such as *Spin, Village Voice, Interview, Trouser Press Guide, Alternative Press, Creem, Rockpool, AllMusicGuide, Ice, Musichound, Emusic, Stereotype, Maximum RocknRoll, Hit List,* and *Amp.* He also regularly blogs at bigtakeover.com. An original late-70s punk rocker/ New York scene member as a teen, hailing from suburban Summit, NJ, he also was (and is now again) the drummer for former early-90s Caroline Records dreampop/shoegaze band Springhouse, who just completed recording their third album. He also drummed for 1980–1984 New York punk band Even Worse (who released an LP retrospective in 2002), and early-00s post-punk group Last Burning Embers (who also released an LP), and toured in 1986 with Los Angeles' SST act Leaving Trains. (He also once sat in for an entire Circle Jerks set in 1983 in New York.) He has been heard regularly on the syndicated radio music show *Music View,* as well as Vancouver's *The Joe Show* and Cincinnati's WOXY. He has appeared in several movie documentaries such as *American Hardcore* and *The Shield Around the K,* and has DJ'd several hundred rock shows (and two regular college radio shows for WJRH and WNYU, where he also hosted the *Pop Quiz* show) in Manhattan since 1979, including the legendary "Rock Hotel" punk shows. After twenty-five years in the East Village of Manhattan, which he now disdains, he lives in Brooklyn, with his wife and cat.
Big Takeover Magazine
1713 8th Ave., Rm. 5-2
Brooklyn, NY 11215
www.bigtakeover.com

Russ Rankin

Russ Rankin was the lead singer for seminal California punk band Good Riddance and currently sings in Only Crime. He is a published poet and a monthly columnist in *AMP* magazine, as well as the writer of several op/ed pieces for magazines such as *Lollipop* and *Alternative Press.* He lives in Santa Cruz, CA.

Jamie Reilly

Jamie Reilly spent the '80s pushing his parents' buttons, the '90s pushing his friends' buttons, and the last fifteen years pushing pixels.

Chris Rest

Chris Rest has played in bands such as RKL and Lagwagon.

Blake Schwarzenbach

Blake Schwarzenbach makes music with words and teaches English at Hunter College, in New York City.

Steven Sciscenti

Steven Sciscenti is a writer living in the San Francisco-Bay area, using the operative pseudonym "Ahi Santiago" for his fiction. His parents were archaeologists, and he spent his childhood shuttling between archaic sites and modern American suburbia. He took a masters degree in fine art from Southern Methodist University in 2002, and was introduced to Wittgensteinian use of language by the director of the Meadows School of the Arts, Jay Sullivan. Subsequent misadventures in sculpture-making convinced Sciscenti to concentrate on writing as his primary creative production. His art criticism articles have been published in the *Donkey Gallery Journal*.

Andrew M. Scott

Andrew M. Scott was born in 1974 in Chicago, IL, and raised in the city's sprawling suburbs. At the age of twelve, an introduction to a wooden plank with four urethane wheels, and the subsequent culture that accompanied it, altered Andrew's life forever. This meeting instilled in him a love for skateboarding, zine making, punk rock, art, and the do-it-yourself ethic. After spending the 1990s feverishly pursuing these things and simultaneously squeezing out a B.A. from the University of Illinois Chicago, he relocated to San Francisco to coordinate *Maximum RocknRoll*.

Following a year-long stint at *MRR*, Andrew opened his own shop in San Francisco's Mission District—a zine, d.i.y. goods, and art gallery by the name of Needles + Pens (currently, in its fifth year of business). Today, in addition to running N+P, Andrew continues to contribute his writing, artwork, and photography to magazines, small press, and skateboard companies. His work has appeared in *Maximum RocknRoll*, *Bail*, *Punk Planet*, the *San Francisco Bay Guardian*, The Yerba Buena Center for the Arts' "Zine Unbound," *Sobstory* (his own sporadically produced zine), and on the bottom of Anti Hero Skateboards. "What are you doing to Participate?"—Big Boys

Andy Shoup

After spending ten years in the hot, dusty, meth-infested city of Modesto, Andy Shoup moved to San Francisco, where he has resided for the last fifteen years. His writing has been published in *Maximum RocknRoll, Heckler*, and *Ain't Nothin' Like Fuckin' Moonshine* magazines, and he edits his own zine, entitled *Connoisseurs of Concrete*. He still loves punk rock and still goes to punk shows.

Ben Sizemore

Ben Sizemore, born in Little Rock, Arkansas, Oct. 23, 1970. Singer for Econochrist, which formed in '88 and disbanded in '93. Currently a social worker in San Francisco, living in Oakland. Still straight edge, still vegetarian, still punk, still pissed off at the man.

Pete Slovenly

Bio? Of me? Peter Menchetti, owner of Sticker Guy! and Slovenly Recordings, originally from New York state, hometown Reno, NV. Been living for the last five years in various European cities... What else would you like to know? www.slovenly.com | www.stickerguy. com | www.myspace.com/slovpete

Shannon Stewart

Shannon Stewart will let people cut in front of her in a traffic jam, but take out anyone who stands in between her and a cup of coffee in the morning. Caught in between the music industry and grass roots organizing, Shannon co-founded the Vera Project in 2001— an all-ages music community center in Seattle, WA—and continued to explore blending community organizing models with what she knows the most about": shows. She now lives in the one area of the country where you can throw a rock and hit a youth organizer/ worker (not that you should of course!), and spends lots of time looking for awesome spaces in unexpected places.

Adam Tanner

Adam Tanner (born 1971) was raised in Western Connecticut along the New York state border.

A high school class sparked his interest in photography and he soon began photographing his friends who were skateboarding, BMX-riding, and starting to play in bands. In late-1987 Adam was brought, by those friends, to a little known club called the Anthrax and there, introduced to the hardcore music scene which would forever change his life.

After a few years of going to concerts at the Anthrax in the late-1980s and traveling from Boston to NYC to DC to see bands play, he began to take his camera to a few shows. Soon he would have that camera at every show he went to, still mostly photographing friends' bands and the more well-known bands they were playing with. Those friends were also putting out their own records, starting record labels, publishing fanzines, and getting interviewed by national magazines.

While going to college in the early-1990s Adam self-published two issues of a magazine called the *Dance of Days* which, while personal, included interviews of bands and all of his own photography. His photography was first published nationally in Revelation Records' *All Ages* book, and he has since worked with *Alternative Press, Rolling Stone, Antimatter, Second Nature, Spin, Skyscraper*, and hundreds of other magazines of varying size and distribution. His photography can be seen in numerous releases by Revelation, Jade Tree, and Victory Records artists, as well as many other band websites and fan sites.

Having photographed thousands of bands, Adam currently resides in Boston, MA. He works in the IT department of an Ivy League school to support his photography addiction and still occasionally photographs some of those "friend's bands."

Michelle Tea

Michelle Tea is the author of *Valencia, Rose of No Man's Land, Chelsea Whistle, Rent Girl, The Beautiful*, and *Passionate Mistakes*. She has edited numerous collections, including *Baby Remember My Name; pills, thrills, chills, and heartache*; and *Without a Net*. Michelle also co-founded the all-girl spoken word troupe Sister Spit and lives in San Francisco.

Trivikrama das

Tim Cohen, aka Trivikrama das, is a professional music therapist and punk musician from the band 108. He was born in NYC, and started going to hardcore punk shows in the early-1980s as a young teenager. His interest in hardcore punk, the occult, and alternative ways of living brought him to explore comparative religion, eastern spirituality, and chanting, which continue to be a focus.

Chris Walter

Chris Walter, a recovering drug addict and hope-to-die punk rocker, began writing purposefully in 1998, when he decided he wanted to leave behind more than a drug-saturated corpse. With help from his girlfriend who works at a printing shop, he started Gofuckyerself Press, and began to write and distribute a series of homemade punk fiction novels. His first published novel *Punk Rules OK* (Burn Books, 2002) went largely unnoticed—except by detractors—and inspired him to return to pirate-style DIY publishing. Now, with thirteen titles, including his latest, *Shouts from the Gutter*, he has expanded his horizons to take on other outlaw authors, including well-known troublemakers Simon Snotface and Australian ne'er-do-well, Drew Gates. He is currently at work on a new book entitled *Rock & Roll Heart.*

Darren Walters

Based in Wilmington, DE, Darren Walters is co-owner of the record label, Jade Tree. He is also is an Adjunct Instructor at Drexel University in the Music Industry Department, rabid soccer player and fan, an avid reader, and prefers Indian cuisine above all else.

Jeremy & Claire Weiss

Jeremy and Claire Weiss are photographers who operate as Day19. Claire was born in Bermuda and Jeremy hails from the state that brought us The Boss. They now split their time between Los Angeles and New York. The two met soon after high school and have been shooting together ever since.

They both attended art school in the shadows of Fenway Park, and shortly after completion headed west to the shadows of Dodger Stadium but they never lost their love for the New York Mets. By growing, learning, and shooting together for over ten years, they have developed a unique sensibility that allows them to capture subjects from complementary perspectives. Clients include Nokia, Dell, Citibank, Dewar's, Island, Virgin, V2, *SOMA, Swindle, Nylon, Anthem, Jane, Elle*, and *Time Out*. They have shown their work in galleries from New York to Los Angeles to Detroit to Portland. Visit them at www.day19.com.

Boff Whalley

Born in Burnley, northern England, at the start of Beatlemania. Grew up in a Mormon family, but swapped it for the Bonzo Dog Doo-Dah Band in early-teens. Punk came along and made sense of everything, so... Dropped out of education, started a band, then another band, and finally a band called Chumbawamba in 1982. Still couldn't play a guitar properly. With seven other like-minds, stuck doggedly to the task ahead and, remarkably, still afloat the good ship Chumbawamba twenty-five years later.

PHOTO CREDITS

P.5 Photo courtesy of Boff Whalley, circa late-seventies

P.8 Naked Raygun photo by Rocco Cipollone, courtesy of Al Quint

P.11 Flyer courtesy of Andy Shoup

P.17 Dickies photo courtesy of Al Quint

P.51 Chapel Hill punks courtesy of Harrison Haynes

P.54 Flyer courtesy of Joseph A. Gervasi

P.59 Agnostic Front photo by BJ Papas, courtesy of Al Quint

P.64 Gang Green photo courtesy of Suburban Voice

P.73 Supertouch photo courtesy of Adam Tanner

P.86 Johnny Ramone, RIP. Photo courtesy of Jeremy & Claire Weiss

P.94 Corrosion on Conformity photo courtesy of Suburban Voice

P.111 Dead Kennedys photo courtesy Suburban Voice

P.115 Gilman flyer courtesy of Craigums

P.119 MDC photo courtesy of Al Quint

P.122–123 Sick of it All photo by BJ Papas, courtesy of Al Quint

P.129 Photo of the Monads courtesy of Michael Azerrad

P.137 Fugazi photo courtesy of Adam Tanner

P.141 Murphy's Law photo courtesy of Suburban Voice

P.149 Jawbreaker photo courtesy of Adam Tanner

P.153 Circle Jerks photo by Cindy Mendes, courtesy of Al Quint

P.157 Political Asylum photo courtesy of Ann Kanaan

P.163 From left: Dan Myes, Stewart Ebersole, Mike Davis, and Allen Milletics, photo
courtesy of Stewart Ebersole

P.173 Al Quint photo by Jed Hresko, courtesy of Al Quint

P.192 Flyer, in all its glory, courtesy of Andy Shoup

P.193 Sean Greene's locker, courtesy of Sean Greene

Clear & Distinct Ideas Presents

D.O.A.

Tales of Terror

Circle Jerks

FAST BACKS

PROBLEM FISH

FRIDAY, MAY 17 TH

7:30 PM

CREST THEATER

1013 K STREET, SACRAMENTO

INFORMATION: 444-3133

Advance Tickets At:
Bass, Ticketron, Tower,
Record Factory, The Beat,
Dimple Records,
Aftermath Records,
Esoteric Records, Spirit
Records

ALSO AVAILABLE FROM AK PRESS

DANIEL COHN-BENDIT & GABRIEL COHN-BENDIT—Obsolete Communism: The Left-Wing Alternative

BENJAMIN DANGL—The Price of Fire: Resource Wars and Social Movements in Bolivia

DARK STAR COLLECTIVE —Beneath the Paving Stones: Situationists and the Beach, May '68

DARK STAR COLLECTIVE —Quiet Rumours: An Anarcha-Feminist Reader

VOLTAIRINE de CLEYRE—Voltarine de Cleyre Reader

CHRIS DUNCAN—My First Time: A Collection of First Punk Show Stories

EG SMITH COLLECTIVE—Animal Ingredients A–Z (3rd edition)

HOWARD EHRLICH—Reinventing Anarchy, Again

SIMON FORD—Realization and Suppression of the Situationist International

BENJAMIN FRANKS—Rebel Alliances

YVES FREMION & VOLNY—Orgasms of History: 3000 Years of Spontaneous Revolt

EMMA GOLDMAN (EDITED BY DAVID PORTER)—Vision on Fire

BERNARD GOLDSTEIN—Five Years in the Warsaw Ghetto

DAVID GRAEBER & STEVPHEN SHUKAITIS—Constituent Imagination

DANIEL GUÉRIN—No Gods No Masters: An Anthology of Anarchism

AGUSTIN GUILLAMÓN—The Friends Of Durruti Group, 1937–1939

ANN HANSEN—Direct Action: Memoirs Of An Urban Guerilla

HELLO—2/15: The Day The World Said NO To War

WILLIAM HERRICK—Jumping the Line: The Adventures and Misadventures of an American Radical

FRED HO—Legacy to Liberation: Politics & Culture of Revolutionary Asian/Pacific America

STEWART HOME—Neoism, Plagiarism & Praxis

STEWART HOME—Neoist Manifestos / The Art Strike Papers

STEWART HOME—No Pity

STEWART HOME—Red London

GEORGY KATSIAFICAS—Subversion of Politics

KATHY KELLY—Other Lands Have Dreams: From Baghdad to Pekin Prison

JAMES KELMAN—Some Recent Attacks: Essays Cultural And Political

KEN KNABB—Complete Cinematic Works of Guy Debord

KATYA KOMISARUK—Beat the Heat: How to Handle Encounters With Law Enforcement

PETER KROPOTKIN—The Conquest of Bread

SAUL LANDAU—A Bus & Botox World

JOSH MACPHEE & ERIK REUHLAND—Realizing the Impossible: Art Against Authority

RICARDO FLORES MAGÓN—Dreams of Freedom: A Ricardo Flores Magón Reader

NESTOR MAKHNO—The Struggle Against The State & Other Essays

SUBCOMANDANTE MARCOS—¡Ya Basta! Ten Years of the Zapatista Uprising

G.A. MATIASZ—End Time

CHERIE MATRIX—Tales From the Clit

ALBERT MELTZER—Anarchism: Arguments For & Against

ALBERT MELTZER—I Couldn't Paint Golden Angels

RAY MURPHY—Siege Of Gresham

NORMAN NAWROCKI—Rebel Moon

MICHAEL NEUMANN—The Case Against Israel

HENRY NORMAL—A Map of Heaven

FIONBARRA O'DOCHARTAIGH—Ulster's White Negroes: From Civil Rights To Insurrection

CRAIG O'HARA—The Philosophy Of Punk

ANTON PANNEKOEK—Workers' Councils

ABEL PAZ (TRANSLATED BY CHUCK MORSE)—Durruti in the Spanish Revolution

BEN REITMAN—Sister of the Road: The Autobiography of Boxcar Bertha

PENNY RIMBAUD—The Diamond Signature
PENNY RIMBAUD—Shibboleth: My Revolting Life
RUDOLF ROCKER—Anarcho-Syndicalism
RUDOLF ROCKER—The London Years
RAMOR RYAN—Clandestines: The Pirate Journals of an Irish Exile
RON SAKOLSKY & STEPHEN DUNIFER—Seizing the Airwaves: A Free Radio Handbook
ROY SAN FILIPPO—A New World In Our Hearts: 8 Years of Writings from the Love and Rage
    Revolutionary Anarchist Federation
MARINA SITRIN—Horizontalism: Voices of Popular Power in Argentina
ALEXANDRE SKIRDA—Facing the Enemy: A History Of Anarchist Organisation From Proudhon To
    May 1968
ALEXANDRE SKIRDA—Nestor Makhno: Anarchy's Cossack
VALERIE SOLANAS—Scum Manifesto
CJ STONE—Housing Benefit Hill & Other Places
ANTONIO TELLEZ—Sabate: Guerilla Extraordinary
MICHAEL TOBIAS—Rage and Reason
JIM TULLY—Beggars of Life: A Hobo Autobiography
TOM VAGUE—Anarchy in the UK: The Angry Brigade
TOM VAGUE—Televisionaries
JAN VALTIN—Out of the Night
RAOUL VANEIGEM—A Cavalier History Of Surrealism
FRANÇOIS EUGENE VIDOCQ—Memoirs of Vidocq: Master of Crime
MARK J. WHITE—An Idol Killing
JOHN YATES—Controlled Flight Into Terrain
JOHN YATES—September Commando
BENJAMIN ZEPHANIAH—Little Book of Vegan Poems
BENJAMIN ZEPHANIAH—School's Out

CDs
MUMIA ABU JAMAL—175 Progress Drive
MUMIA ABU JAMAL—All Things Censored Vol.1
MUMIA ABU JAMAL—Spoken Word
JUDI BARI—Who Bombed Judi Bari?
JELLO BIAFRA—Become the Media
JELLO BIAFRA—Beyond The Valley of the Gift Police
JELLO BIAFRA—The Big Ka-Boom, Part One
JELLO BIAFRA—High Priest of Harmful
JELLO BIAFRA—I Blow Minds For A Living
JELLO BIAFRA—In the Grip of Official Treason
JELLO BIAFRA—If Evolution Is Outlawed
JELLO BIAFRA—Machine Gun In The Clown's Hand
JELLO BIAFRA—No More Cocoons
NOAM CHOMSKY—An American Addiction
NOAM CHOMSKY—Case Studies in Hypocrisy
NOAM CHOMSKY—Emerging Framework of World Power
NOAM CHOMSKY—Free Market Fantasies
NOAM CHOMSKY—The Imperial Presidency
NOAM CHOMSKY—New War On Terrorism: Fact And Fiction
NOAM CHOMSKY—Propaganda and Control of the Public Mind

NOAM CHOMSKY—Prospects for Democracy
NOAM CHOMSKY & CHUMBAWAMBA—For A Free Humanity: For Anarchy
CHUMBAWAMBA—A Singsong and A Scrap
WARD CHURCHILL—Doing Time: The Politics of Imprisonment
WARD CHURCHILL—In A Pig's Eye: Reflections on the Police State, Repression, and Native America
WARD CHURCHILL—Life in Occupied America
WARD CHURCHILL—Pacifism and Pathology in the American Left
ALEXANDER COCKBURN—Beating the Devil
ANGELA DAVIS—The Prison Industrial Complex
THE EX—1936: The Spanish Revolution
NORMAN FINKELSTEIN—An Issue of Justice: Origins of the Israel/Palestine Conflict
ROBERT FISK—War, Journalism, and the Middle East
FREEDOM ARCHIVES—Chile: Promise of Freedom
FREEDOM ARCHIVES—Prisons on Fire: George Jackson, Attica & Black Liberation
FREEDOM ARCHIVES—Robert F. Williams: Self-Defense, Self-Respect & Self-Determination
JAMES KELMAN—Seven Stories
TOM LEONARD—Nora's Place and Other Poems 1965–99
CASEY NEILL—Memory Against Forgetting
GREG PALAST—Live From the Armed Madhouse
GREG PALAST—Weapon of Mass Instruction
CHRISTIAN PARENTI—Taking Liberties
UTAH PHILLIPS—I've Got To know
UTAH PHILLIPS—Starlight on the Rails box set
DAVID ROVICS—Behind the Barricades: Best of David Rovics
ARUNDHATI ROY—Come September
VARIOUS—Better Read Than Dead
VARIOUS—Less Rock, More Talk
VARIOUS—Mob Action Against the State: Collected Speeches from the Bay Area Anarchist Bookfair
VARIOUS—Monkeywrenching the New World Order
VARIOUS—Return of the Read Menace
HOWARD ZINN—Artists In A Time of War
HOWARD ZINN—Heroes and Martyrs: Emma Goldman, Sacco & Vanzetti, and the Revolutionary
     Struggle
HOWARD ZINN—A People's History of the United States: A Lecture at Reed
HOWARD ZINN—People's History Project Box Set
HOWARD ZINN—Stories Hollywood Never Tells

DVDs
NOAM CHOMSKY—Imperial Grand Strategy: The Conquest of Iraq and the Assault on Democracy
NOAM CHOMSKY—Distorted Morality
STEVEN FISCHLER & JOEL SUCHER—Anarchism in America/Free Voice of Labor
ARUNDHATI ROY—Instant-Mix Imperial Democracy
ROZ PAYNE ARCHIVES—What We Want, What We Believe: The Black Panther Party Library (4 DVD
     set)
HOWARD ZINN & ANTHONY ARNOVE (ed.)—Readings from Voices of a People's History of the
     United States

FRIENDS OF AK PRESS

Help sustain our vital project!

AK Press is a worker-run collective that publishes and distributes radical books, audio/visual media, and other material. We're small: a dozen individuals who work long hours for short money, because we believe in what we do. We're anarchists, which is reflected both in the books we publish and the in the way we organize our business: without bosses.

AK Press publishes the finest books, CDs, and DVDs from the anarchist and radical traditions—currently about 18 to 20 per year. Joining The Friends of AK Press is a way in which you can directly help us to keep the wheels rolling and these important projects coming.

As ever, money is tight as we do not rely on outside funding. We need your help to make and keep these crucial materials available. Friends pay a minimum (of course we have no objection to larger sums!) of $20/£15 per month, for a minimum three month period. Money received goes directly into our publishing funds. In return, Friends automatically receive (for the duration of their membership), as they appear, one FREE copy of EVERY new AK Press title. Secondly, they are also entitled to a 10% discount on EVERY-THING featured in the AK Press distribution catalog—or on our website—on ANY and EVERY order. We also have a program where individuals or groups can sponsor a whole book.

PLEASE CONTACT US FOR MORE DETAILS:

AK Press
674-A 23rd Street
Oakland, CA 94612
akpress@akpress.org
www.akpress.org

AK Press
PO Box 12766
Edinburgh, Scotland EH8, 9YE
ak@akedin.demon.co.uk
www.akuk.com